MW01274137

Crime
Punishment
Power

SOCIOLOGICAL EXPLANATIONS

Jeffrey Shantz
Kwantlen Polytechnic University

Kendall Hunt
publishing company

Cover image © 2012 Jeffrey Shantz

Kendall Hunt
publishing company

www.kendallhunt.com
Send all inquiries to:
4050 Westmark Drive
Dubuque, IA 52004-1840

Copyright © 2012 by Kendall Hunt Publishing Company

ISBN 978-0-7575-9791-6

Printed in the United States of America
10 9 8 7 6 5 4 3 2

CONTENTS

Chapter 9

Chapter 10

Chapter 11

Chapter 12

References

Developing a Sociological Imagination

What is deviance? What is crime? What is it that makes some activities deviant or criminal while other, perhaps more harmful activities are viewed as normal or acceptable. These are among the questions that concern criminologists.

Deviance refers to behaviors that depart from social norms and accepted ways of acting. Such behaviors are not necessarily uncommon. Even more, they are not necessarily negative acts. One thing is consistent about deviance. Everybody does it. Everyone reading this text, everyone in this class is a deviant. You may not be ready to admit it. You may not want to hear it. But you are a deviant. Everyone has committed a deviant act. Criminologist Thomas Gabor suggests that "crime is more like the common cold — an affliction to which no one is immune but to which everyone is not equally susceptible" (1994, 6). If everyone is a deviant, or even a criminal, why do we not view ourselves as a deviant or criminal? Why do we only tend to impose these identities on others?

The notion of deviance implies that there is an acceptance of norms that people may or may not agree with. Yet, there are typically many differing views about what acts constitute crime or deviance. One's perspective is very much related to one's position or status within society, with the experiences and needs of one's particular community. Notions of consensus mask great differences, debates, and divergences in perspective.

Definitions of deviance and crime change over time and across cultures. Definitions of actions as deviant or criminal may be based on morals and values that are not widely shared. You can probably think of a variety of issues that are defined on the basis of morals and values that not everyone would agree with. Some of these issues will be defined as deviant, others as criminal. This definition occurs not because everyone, or even a majority of people, agrees with it but, rather, because enough people with authority agreed with it and were able to assign a label of deviance or criminality and were able to make that label stick.

A few examples of issues around which there is much debate and controversy regarding whether or not the activity is acceptable or unacceptable, legal or illegal, include: sex work; same sex marriage, abortion, stem cell research, polygamy, and euthanasia. Perceptions of these issues, and the values associated with them, can rapidly change depending on changes in the social order.

One of the issues around which there has been a great deal of change in societal perspectives, in only the last thirty or so years, is the issue of gambling and, relatedly, casinos. As recently as the early 1990s, gambling, and especially gambling in casinos, was viewed largely as a rather seedy, undesirable, and even degenerate behavior. It was something to be restricted to specific tourist areas, such as Las Vegas or Atlantic City, not something people wanted in their own towns. Indeed, cities associated with gambling, like Vegas, were themselves viewed as rather seedy locations that one might visit but certainly would not reside. By the mid 1990s, when proposals were put forward to place casinos in Canadian cities, such as Windsor, Ontario, there was strong and loud opposition from various community groups who fought to keep casinos, and later video gaming terminals, out of the city. Many feared that casinos would lead to a degradation of the city and particularly downtown areas near proposed casino sites. By the end of the 1990s, however, attitudes had changed dramatically. By mid 2000s, casino proposals generated little public opposition. In 2011, cities are as likely to fight to get a casino, as a source of revenue and jobs, as they are to oppose it in any way. In the course of a couple of decades an issue has gone from being viewed overwhelmingly as deviant or criminal to being largely accepted, even, in some cases, desirable.

One might suggest that killing someone is always wrong and will always be treated as such within society. Even in that case, there is no absolute consensus about such a drastic and dramatic event. What about self defense? What about killing during wars? Canada has been at war in Afghanistan for almost a decade. Should Canadian soldiers be regarded with revulsion or charged with crimes for killing people in Afghanistan? Have they been? Are they?

Chapter 1: Developing a Sociological Imagination

One of the key processes that criminologists need to understand is the way in which the norms of elite groups are passed off as common or shared by society as a whole. In times of war states are not likely to criminalize even horrendous acts committed by the people they have mobilized to carry out a war and occupation. They are more likely to criminalize and punish the protesters and critics who oppose or question war and occupation.

Criminologists need to understand the processes and practices by which acts that are simply different, some even harmless, are constructed as deviant. They must understand how acts perceived as deviant come to be viewed and treated as criminal. Who gets to decide? Why? How was it determined who decides? Who benefits from such processes and practices? Why is it that more harmful acts, even deadly acts, never come to be viewed as deviant or criminal?

At the heart of these processes and practices are exertions of power. Some assert and secure the capacity to decide. Some get to define social problems and have their definitions stick on society while others are never heard, their definitions do not take hold socially.

Absolutist and Constructionist Perspectives on Social Problems

What is it about specific problems in our society that makes them "social"? Why do we refer to certain concerns as "social problems"? First, problems are social because they have broader impacts beyond those immediately involved. They are more than personal. Their harms involve multiple individuals and groups in society and they have far reaching effects. Second, they are social because there is broad public interest and concern about the issue. It forms the subject of public discourse, debate, and action. Third, problems are social because they cannot be solved by one or two individuals alone. Addressing issues like global climate change or industrial pollution requires collective action involving individuals and groups from a range of social positions. You might, as an individual, wish to correct the problem but you will not be able to without the work of others. Large scale collective mobilizations may be necessary to address the issue effectively.

In broad terms there are two primary overarching frameworks through which social problems, deviance, and crime are viewed and discussed. These frameworks might be termed the absolutist and the constructionist. Powerful institutions, such as the mass media and government tend to adopt absolutist approaches to social problems. Constructionist approaches are preferred within many community organizations. Constructionist approaches also inform much theory and practice in sociology. These broad frameworks can be distinguished according to a few key features characterizing each.

The first feature is the way in which each framework explains the causation of social problems, crime, or deviance. Absolutist approaches tend to offer a unicausal explanation of social problems, emphasizing one primary or dominant factor said to cause criminal activity. For absolutists, the singular explanation usually focuses on factors relating to the individual, such as personality disorders, upbringing, or character flaws. Constructionist approaches tend to be multicausal, identifying various factors that can contribute to criminal activity. Such factors might include the economic climate, political decisions, cultural factors, opportunity structures as well as individual proclivities.

The second feature relates to the way in which possible responses or solutions to crime are viewed. Absolutists tend to offer singular responses to crime or deviance and these singular responses tend to be punitive. Thus, for absolutists, the primary solution pursued in dealing with crime is tougher "law and order" legislation, stiffer penalties, and increased incarceration. More police and more prisons, in other words. Constructionists tend to offer multiple responses for dealing with social problems. In the case of homelessness for example, while absolutists have emphasized legislation and policing practices that target homeless people for criminalization, constructionists focus on employment, affordable housing, health care, and social assistance as multiple components of an effective response to the problem.

The third feature refers to the general orientation to society and authorities within society that each approach upholds. Absolutists tend to be authoritarian, both in how they define social problems and in how they respond to them. Absolutists accept statist definitions of crime and deviance. Something is a problem because the state has identified it as such. If some activity is "against the law" then it must be a problematic activity. Absolutists condemn people for "breaking the law" but tend not to question whether or not the law itself is unjust or inappropriate. They do not question the inequalities that exist between those who get to make laws, typically elites, and those who are subjected to laws, typically non-elites. At the same time absolutists are authoritarian in their response to social problems. Typically their response is to rely on authorities. Call the police. Ask politicians to address the issue through legislation or resources. Let the authorities take care of it and do not get directly involved. Constructionists, on the other hand, tend to be participatory in their approach to explaining and responding to social problems. They prefer to define social problems according to actual, real harms done, and the specific needs of communities involved or affected. Thus, constructionists might note that the criminal justice system spends far too much money, time, resources, and personnel on harmless or nuisance activities, such as squeegeeing, squatting, or graffiti that predominantly bother only elites, such as business owners; while giving almost no attention or resources to devastatingly harmful activities, such as toxic waste dumping, workplace exploitation, greenhouse gas emissions, or occupational health and safety, that may benefit elites while leading to numerous injuries, illnesses, and death for non-elites. Constructionists also prefer a participatory approach in dealing with social problems. Rather than relying on authorities, they prefer to organize within their communities to find direct, local solutions that respond to and meet the needs of the people involved. Examples might include restorative justice or community clinics.

Finally, it can be said that for absolutists the primary emphasis is on placing blame. Absolutists target specific groups or individuals who are then blamed for societal problems. Groups that have been typically identified for blame by absolutists include gang members, drug users, welfare recipients, homeless people, youth, subcultures such as punk or hip hop, and sex workers. Often people have been identified on the basis of ethnic or racial background or sexual identity. In unequal and socially stratified societies, where there are elites and non-elites, wealthy and poor, not everyone is able to assign blame equally. Control of blame represents a tremendous power. In stratified, class-based societies like Canada and the United States, blame is almost always wielded in a downward direction. Those who wield economic and political power, such as corporate owners and politicians, are able to place blame on those who lack power. Those who lack power are more likely to be blamed for social problems and to be punished. For example, unemployment is blamed on lazy or unskilled working people who supposedly will not take lousy jobs rather than on corporate executives who lay people off or close down and move workplaces to save on labour costs and raise their own corporate bonuses, or politicians that give out corporate grants and then sign trade agreements that allow companies to move in search of cheaper labour without meeting local obligations. To focus on elites, the executives or politicians, would be to wield blame in an upward direction.

Rather than assigning blame, constructionists prefer to seek understanding. Assigning blame is easy. Any less powerful group can easily be identified and have blame, labels, or stigma attached to them. They lack the means to fend off negative attributions. But blame does not improve situations. It does not offer a solution. Incarceration does not reduce crime. Societies like the U.S., with the highest incarceration rates also have the worst crime rates, and those rates tend to increase as the punishment increases. In order to effect positive change in society it is necessary to develop understanding, to realize and address the complex relationships and practices that give rise to social problems. Only then can longer term, durable solutions to problems be implemented. Understanding does not mean excusing, however. People are still held accountable for their actions, but in ways that recognize and address the various factors that contribute to social problems rather than being satisfied with affixing blame. The work of sociology is largely the work of developing understanding.

In Canada and the United States, the response to social problems is focused largely on so-called "pathological individuals" who, because of some personal problem, failing, or pathology, inflict harm on people or society. Responsibility for social problems is placed overwhelmingly on individuals. For example, responsibility for poverty is placed largely on the poor and their imagined "lifestyles." The language used is often moralizing in tone, using language of accusation and condemnation. Poor people are called lazy, careless, or irresponsible. They are accused of imagined violations such as welfare fraud. Such approaches once again emphasize blame rather than understanding.

Crime is an important election issue. The focus on crime has become, in the twenty-first century, a key issue for all parties. Perhaps for the first time all parties, including the social democratic New Democratic Party (NDP), are competing with each other to see which will be toughest on crime.

The Sociological Imagination

In order to get beyond individualistic responses to social problems we need to develop a sociological imagination. The sociological imagination is a term developed by the sociologist C. Wright Mills in the late 1950s. Through the sociological imagination, one is able to recognize and understand the interplay of social structures and individual lives. Mills presented the sociological imagination as a way to help individuals to better understand their relationships within social structures and institutions, and to appreciate more fully their experiences within broader ongoing historical transformations.

According to Mills: "neither the life of an individual nor the history of society can be understood without understanding both" (1959, ii). Without such an integrated understanding, social problems in society cannot be adequately and effectively addressed, and people have difficulty escaping unsatisfactory situations and transforming their lives and society for the better.

The period following World War II was a time of great social, economic, political, and cultural upheaval. Millions of people had their lives disrupted or devastated by the war. At the same time, the period after the war was a period of economic growth as expanding industrial production saw a growth in stable, better paying jobs. Cities and communities were transformed as new workers, many from outside areas with vastly different cultural histories, moved to the urban centres in search of the newly opening jobs while simultaneously, upwardly mobile workers left behind older residential areas inside the cities for new homes in the newly developed suburbs.

The result was that many people found themselves feeling trapped by the multiple pressures of unemployment, job searches, work, family needs, and the uncertainty or unfamiliarity of city or suburban life in changing environments in which they may have few connections with neighbours.

At the same time people also felt growing pressures to succeed economically, to "make it" or realize "the American Dream" of financial success — a dream that was not available to everyone. Along with this pressure to succeed was the associated sense that if one did not succeed and realize the American Dream, it was solely because of some personal or individual failing or deficiency on their part. Once again social issues, like unemployment or poverty, became individualized as personal troubles, like not trying hard enough or being lazy. Added to the pressure of trying to succeed was the threat that you would be viewed as a loser or a failure, regardless of how hard you actually worked or tried to better yourself. Coupled with rapid, seemingly uncontrollable, social change, one is left with a sense of being powerless to change the society or one's place within it. Such tensions, mixed with frustration, can lead to harmful conflicts and negative behaviors that serve neither to better society nor oneself.

By developing the notion of the sociological imagination, Mills sought to provide people with some tools to assist them and their associates, to get beyond the feeling of being trapped in society. First he draws a distinction between personal troubles and public issues. Public issues are social problems — those occurrences, events, or troubles that arise from social, economic, political, or environmental structures or institutional practices. Examples might include economic depressions, political repression, ecological destruction, or war. Personal troubles are the individual experiences of turmoil, strife, or social dissatisfaction that pose challenges for people in uniquely felt ways. The sociological imagination encourages us to see that what appear, on the surface, to be private difficulties of the individual have direct links with broader social structures. To properly understand the issues, we must be able to get past the surface appearance to see the direct, but often deeper, connections in social relationships and societal institutions and practices.

To understand the meaningful and significant connections between personal troubles and public issues, Mills refers to the example of unemployment. In a city of 100,000 people, if there is only one person unemployed, it might be said that this can be understood as a personal trouble related to the personality, interests, character, or skills of that person and/or the opportunities immediately available to him or her. The solution to the issue might be relatively straightforward in terms of assistance or relief as well. However, if in a city of 100,000 people, 10,000 are unemployed, this is a public issue. It will not be understood properly by looking at the personal characteristics or opportunities available for any one individual. It will not likely be possible to examine the personal circumstances of all the individuals and such an examination would be lacking. For Mills, under such circumstances of mass unemployment, the entire opportunity structure itself in society has collapsed. In situations such as this, both understanding the issue and addressing it effectively will require analysis of the social, economic, and political structures and institutions in the society. Solutions will require more than relief or donations to an individual or individuals but a broader transformation of social relations themselves.

One could take a similar approach to understand and discuss poverty and homelessness. In advanced industrial capitalist countries like Canada and the U.S., poverty and homelessness are attributed largely to personal troubles, character faults or failings, such as laziness, lack of education or training, decreased willpower, mental illness, or substance abuse. Poverty and homelessness are portrayed as personal troubles and the links to social structures, such as economic recession, labour market changes, policy transformations, trade agreements, lack of affordable housing stock, and workplace closures, are ob-

Chapter 1: Developing a Sociological Imagination

scured. Governments in states and provinces in the U.S. and Canada have responded to poverty and homelessness largely as if they are deviant or criminal behaviors to be punished through increased policing, tougher laws, and even incarceration. In Ontario and British Columbia, for example, governments have introduced legislation, the Safe Streets Act, that criminalizes the survival strategies of homeless people, such as squeegee cleaning car windshields and panhandling. In those provinces the governments have also pursued legislation that would allow the police to forcibly remove homeless people from the streets and place them in shelters or jails.

The sociological imagination can help to inform social policy and community development. It provides a useful alternative to absolutist approaches in government and media that, rather than understanding social problems, serve largely to blame individuals who are experiencing those problems. Instead of treating poverty and homelessness as individual problems or as acts of personal deviance or crime as many governments do currently, including governments in British Columbia and Ontario, the sociological imagination would encourage a proper understanding of poverty and homelessness as that which they are — social problems with structural and institutional causes and structural solutions.

In addressing issues, no matter how narrow or specific or broad and complex they might be, from the perspective of a sociological imagination, the inquisitive researcher should ask three primary questions according to Mills. These questions are hallmarks of any critical analysis.

The first question posed by Mills asks: "What is the structure of the particular society as a whole?" This question inquires after the social order. Is the society hierarchical, with great differences between those with resources and those without or is the society more horizontal and egalitarian? What are the major components of the society and how are they related?

The second question asks: "Where does the society stand in human history?" Is it a feudal society or a modern one? Is it a new society emerging following a period of revolution or war or is it an older, more tradition-based society that has not changed much for generations? Is it a colonizing society or one that is colonized? How does the society relate to other societies in the same period? How are the features of the society in question affected by the historical period? What are the mechanisms by which the society is changing? Is it rapid, dramatic change or slow, gradual change?

The third question is perhaps the least straightforward, but at the same time maybe the most interesting. It queries: "What are the varieties of men and women that inhabit the society in the period in question?" On one level this might refer to demographic issues, such as age, sex, gender, sexuality, or class. This is useful information that might help the researcher to answer some questions. Most arrests involve younger males, for example. Yet, Mills means something more philosophical and complex in asking this question. He is really asking, what sorts of characteristics or attributes are being selected and privileged within a specific society? How is human nature understood in a particular society? In market based, competitive societies human nature is likely to be described as competitive, "dog eat dog," or cutthroat. In coopera- tive societies based on shared resources, human nature is likely to be viewed as cooperative or collective. Societies engaged in warlike activities are more likely to view human nature as violent or warlike. Human nature comes from the varying contexts of social relations, it is not at all natural or constant across different societies. The ways that people describe human nature will tell you a good deal about the sort of society in which they live. Changing perceptions of human nature will tell you about important changes in the society.

The individual is a product of specific, multiple, and overlapping historical forces. These forces involve economics, politics, culture, geography, and ecol- ogy. Mills argues that the sociological imagination allows one to see the re- lations between history, broad social processes, and biography, the intimate life situation of the individual. As the sociologist John Berger suggests, it is the capacity to see the general in the particular. Each person in society is unique, but we carry with us characteristics of the economy, politics, culture, geography, and history of the society or societies in which we live. For ex- ample, in a warlike society we may be marked by a tolerance for violence. In a misogynist society that treats women unequally, we may be marked by the mistreatment of women or devaluation of their labour. In a class-based soci- ety, we may accept poverty in our midst. This can even affect how we come to view human nature and the character of the species. For example, in a com- petitive, market-based society, people may believe that aggressive competition and winner-take-all attitudes are simply normal parts of human nature rather than byproducts of a particular social order that values competitive struggle. Yet in other cooperatively organized societies, like many gather-hunter societ- ies, aggressive competition would be viewed as pathological or deviant and would, because of scarce resources, pose a very real threat to society. In such cooperatively-based societies human nature would be understood instead as primarily cooperative. Thus, even notions of what is natural, or human nature, are based largely on the type of social structure in which we live. The general, or social, is expressed in the particular, or individual.

For Mills, it is crucial that people understand the interactions of their own lives with society, its structures and institutions. Otherwise tensions between personal troubles and public issues cannot be overcome positively. According to Mills, people feel trapped because "their visions and their powers are limited to the close-up scenes of job, family, neighbourhood" (1959, 3). They cannot see the forest for the trees, so to speak. Because they are so wrapped up in their immediate lives, people cannot see clearly the larger sociological processes and patterns in which their lives are embedded.

The sociological imagination is not simply a specific theory or concept. Rather it is a broader orientation to the world. It is a way of positioning oneself within society and its social relationships. The sociological imagination refers to practices of probing and questioning the taken-for-granted aspects of social life. For Mills, the sociological imagination is a "quality of mind" that helps them to situate themselves within social relationships. This orientation to the world aids people in understanding social history and personal biography, and the relations between the two within the context of specific societies.

Mills was of the view that most people, because they are caught up in the day to day demands of work, school, and/or family, "do not possess the quality of mind essential to grasp the interplay of man and society, of biography and history, of self and world" (1959, 4). Yet, anyone could, with a little support and assistance, develop such an orientation. Sociology, by offering some theoretical and practical guideposts, could play a part in nurturing such a quality of mind.

Sociologists recognize a subjective element in the definition of social problems. Aspects of power and inequality, including along lines of gender, race, ethnicity, class, sexuality, and so forth, are involved in the construction of social problems. Definitions of social problems depend on the moral and social stances of those who do the defining. Social constructionists look at the process and manner by which people construct images and definitions of social problems. They focus on intersubjective processes of creating and defining social problems. At the same time individuals have some ability to influence events.

Critical Perspectives on Crime

Crime is often viewed as external to us. It is something that other people do. Focusing on extreme crimes serves to distance so-called citizens from so-called "criminals." Everyday conceptions of deviance and crime have been focused on people who share the trait of powerlessness. Recent examples within a North American context include: sex workers, drug dealers, welfare recipients, "squeegee kids," and the addicted. Everyday conceptions of deviance and crime tend not to focus on elites and the more privileged, such as corporate polluters, financial speculators, and arms dealers, even though they inflict much greater harm on individuals and society than do non-elite "street criminals." Indeed, elites who engage in harmful and dangerous activities may be celebrated as "leading citizens," role models, or economically productive members of society.

From a critical perspective notions of deviance, and the identification of less powerful members of society with deviant labels, are connected with relations and structures of power. This occurs in multiple ways within advanced industrial capitalist societies. For one thing, the norms and laws in industrial societies reflect, and even express, the interests, values, preoccupations and preferences of economic, political, social, and cultural elites. Those people who pose a threat to elite interests, either by redistributing property or advocating for a more egalitarian and cooperative society, come to be labelled as radicals, malcontents, troublemakers, thieves, or bandits.

Beyond this, even when the behaviors of elites is questioned, they have the resources — in the media, legal professionals, politicians, and public relations firms — to deflect or counter deviant labels. Corporate executives who order the dumping of toxic wastes or who fail to ensure safe workplaces are rarely identified publicly and held personally accountable for their actions in the way that a shoplifter or car thief would be.

Even more, the belief that norms and laws are natural, good, and shared masks their political character. We might, at times, question how the laws are applied in specific cases, but we rarely question whether or not the laws themselves are necessarily unjust or unfair.

This suggests that any particular act may or may not be considered deviant at a given moment or period in time. It may not be inherently deviant. What makes something deviant is whether or not it is defined as such and how people then respond to it. Crucially, crime and deviance do not result solely from the actions of an offender, but also from the responses of conforming members of society.

From a sociological perspective, conforming members of society play three key interrelated roles. First, they establish the rules. Second, they enforce the rules. Third, they provide deviant identities to those caught violating the rules. Notions of deviance and crime result from interactions among conforming members of society. Thus, sociologists are concerned not only with the circumstances that lead people to violate rules, but also with the transactions by which people and their actions become defined as deviant.

Rules in society do not simply arise automatically in response to some obvious, apparent, or "natural" need. Rules emerge because someone takes initiative and pushes for their enactment. As we will see in this book, the sociologist Howard Becker refers to these people as "moral entrepreneurs."

Before becoming Prime Minister of Canada, William Lyon Mackenzie King, a civil servant, acted as a moral entrepreneur for privileged groups demanding harsher narcotics laws. The main lobbyists pushing for the laws were based in Vancouver and their real motivation was not halting drug use but regulating Chinese immigrants. The Opium Act of 1908 outlawed trafficking, but because of difficulties catching someone in the act of selling, lobbyists demanded bans on possession and personal use as well. A publicity campaign calling for tougher laws made use of racist stereotypes and fear mongering against Asian migrants, depicting Chinese men as preying upon white women. The campaign was successful. In 1911 possession was outlawed and enforcement given over to the Royal Canadian Mounted Police (RCMP), who at the time were on the verge of being disbanded. Notably only those of poor and insecure social and economic status were criminalized, not doctors and their more privileged patients, many of whom could have been described as addicts.

Criminal (In)Justice Systems

Understanding the role of power in the social construction of crime and deviance raises important questions about the systems, structures, and institutions that have been developed to address crime and deviance. Can a justice system be truly just within a social organization where fundamental social inequalities exist? What is presented as criminal justice is often not just.

Unequal power relations within society are disguised by consensus notions of crime. Consensus perspectives on crime suggest that people have equal opportunity to pursue rewards that are not distributed equally. One example cited as evidence of consensus in societies like Canada and the U.S. is the fact that everyone of voting age can participate in the political process. Not everyone's choice will succeed and win the election but all can participate equally to pursue the goal.

From a critical perspective, society is structured by class, race, ethnicity, gender, age, and sexuality, with uneven and unequal opportunities for people depending on their location within the structure of identities and relationships. Conflict approaches, influenced by Marxism or anarchism, suggest that complex societies are characterized by battles of deviance and social control. In the outcome of these battles winners gain the privilege of organizing social life and the losers find themselves trapped by the social vision of others. Notions of crime have class bases throughout. For critical criminologists, the state is a mechanism of social control with the criminal justice system a key part of that mechanism. The criminal justice system, rather than securing justice "for all," reproduces social inequality and social injustice.

Some sociologists suggest that law enforcement causes crime. To be sure, you will find crime where you look for it. High crime rates in certain areas may result largely, or even solely, from the expectation by authorities that they will find it there. By searching on the basis of their pre-conceived notions they, in effect, create a "self-fulfilling prophecy." As well, police sometimes aggravate public disorder through their own violence, as we see when we look at policing of protests and demonstrations. In numerous cases, including the 1997 APEC protests at the University of British Columbia and the G8/G20 protests in Toronto in 2010, police can create disruptive situations simply by attacking otherwise peaceful protesters.

Critical theorists sometimes make the distinction between social control and moral regulation. Social control is often equated with state repression and punishment. This includes the deployment of laws, customs, rules, regulations, surveillance, and restrictions. Means of social control usually refer to planned and programmed responses to expected and realized deviance rather than the broader, general institutions of society that produce conformity in people's everyday lives. It involves organized social responses.

Critical theorists are quick to point out that the state does not have total control. People are also subjected to social control within public and private spheres beyond the state. Social control involves, and deploys, underlying moral precepts. There is a connection between law and morality. Where do assumptions about "normalcy" and "deviance" come from, for example?

Along with social control through repression, criminologists often speak also of moral regulation as a mechanism for shaping people's behavior. Moral regulation establishes what is right and wrong, acceptable and unacceptable, often through informal mechanisms such as public shaming, condemnation and chastisement, and ostracizing or shunning. Moral regulation encourages certain forms of conduct and expression while discouraging others. It establishes disciplinary regimes, including systems of social reward and punishment. Moral regulation forms identities and shapes "conduct and conscience through self-appropriation of morals and beliefs about what is right and wrong, possible and impossible, normal and pathological" (Rousmaniere, Dehli, and de Coninck-Smith, 1997, 5). Critical theorists argue that we must always ask who is doing the regulating and who is being regulated. Whose values in society are viewed as moral and proper? On the other hand, whose behaviors are viewed as being wrong or unacceptable?

Moral regulation imposes the boundaries of "normal" in society. It operates like a net that is at once "restrictive, yet full of holes" (Strange and Loo 1997, 5). Moral regulation is at play in almost every sphere of state practice. It occurs through taxation (cigarette taxes, tax money used for unwanted wars), financing (decisions about corporate grants or welfare expenditures), citizenship (business class or family class), and the criminal justice system itself (bylaw enforcement, anti-panhandling laws). The modern state itself grew through increasing involvement and interference in expanding areas of social activity.

In addition to the state, moral regulation occurs through the medical profession, psychology, and psychiatry. It also occurs through social reform movements such as the anti-smoking movement, alcohol prohibition movements, and movements against gambling.

Social theorist Michel Foucault expands notions of moral regulation to speak of the processes in which people come to govern themselves. His term governmentality refers to the way in which people internalize the moral codes of various social agents, whether government officials, media spokespeople, civic leaders, or religious figures, to govern themselves and shape their own conduct. The term can be broken down to give the sense that people govern their own mentality or mental processes.

CHAPTER 2

Ruling Ideas: From Demonic Possession to Social Contract

Ideas are intimately connected to relations of power. Power allows for the promotion of some ideas while providing means to silence or erase others. The political economist Karl Marx once suggested that: "the ideas of the ruling class are in every epoch the ruling ideas, i.e. the class which is the ruling *material* force of society, is, at the same time, its ruling *intellectual* force" (1970, 64). Marx offers this analysis in his book *The German Ideology* (1845), in an attempt to explain why German philosophy of his day tended to echo or reinforce the worldviews and prejudices of ruling social elites. Marx is pointing out that there are no value-free ideas. Ideas, and schools of thought more broadly, are selected, promoted, and defended by specific social actors, including groups and organizations, that motivate for and mobilize support for certain ideas over others on the basis of their own particular interests and objectives.

In class based societies, like contemporary Canadian and U.S. societies, those with access to wealth and resources — who control media channels like Rupert Murdoch and Suncorp or broader cultural productions like Disney — are largely able to determine what ideas are heard and circulated. Typically these are ideas that support the interests of the power holders themselves. At the same time power holders can ensure that opposing or alternative ideas — the ideas of social reformers, union organizers, or activists — are rarely heard. Even more they can present distorted versions of these ideas in order to discredit them. This happens often in reports of protests against capitalist globalization and the alternative globalization movements, for example. Meanwhile those who lack resources — who do not own and control media channels —

will have a great difficulty getting alternative, even more informative, ideas out to a wider audience. Thus, ruling ideas will tend to be the ideas that best represent and flatter dominant groups.

The chapter begins by situating modern theories in the late medieval and early modern periods, examining the emergence of criminological theory in the collapse of feudal structures and the rise of capitalist political and economic systems. The chapter examines religious perspectives on crime and punishment — the demonic viewpoints that dominated medieval and early modern approaches and justified feudal hierarchies — and the emergence of philosophical theories of criminology in the tumultuous uproar of the early periods in the rise and establishment of capitalist social, economic, and political systems.

Throughout, the argument is made that theories, of any sort, can only be properly understood and discussed by analyzing the social relations: conflict, status, class, inequalities, and interests; and structures: government, capital, nation; in which the theories are developed, proposed, received, and accepted or rejected. Criminology, as for other theories, reflects the relations of power and inequality that exist in the society more broadly within which the theories are developed. Often the "best" or most useful and accurate theories are not the ones that are popularized, disseminated, and discussed, while "crank" theories that offer few insights or have no basis in real world circumstances become dominant and circulate widely. Often theories are selected only because they support the powerful and are rejected solely because they challenge or disturb social elites.

Context Matters

As C. Wright Mills suggests, developing a sociological imagination requires attention to historical context. In order to understand the emergence and proliferation of idea systems and schools of thought, it is necessary to situate these ideas within specific structures and relationships. Different historical periods exhibit distinct cultural and social practices based on levels of economic and technological development. Ideas are produced and distributed differently depending on whether the society has printing presses or not, for example. Communication occurs differently in an era of global satellite systems than in a period of telegraph wires.

Similarly, and more important, different eras are marked by distinct power relations and structures of rule. Capitalist societies are marked by vastly greater disparities in wealth and control of resources than are seen in gatherer-hunter societies in which people have relatively equal access to resources.

Thus, if one wants properly to understand crime and punishment — and popular or dominant ideas about crime and punishment — it is necessary to specify what social context or society one is talking about. If one wants to understand modern issues of crime and punishment, one must understand social relations, structures, and institutions that shape modern societies — what is sometimes called modernity — and how these modern conditions emerged and under what conditions they are established and maintained.

Even academic disciplines like psychology, sociology, or criminology in the West, which claim to be objective, value-free, and universal, emerge in periods of turmoil such as those that accompanied the collapse of feudalism and the rise of capitalist society. The disciplines are marked by conflict and reflect competing interests within social development. To understand properly these disciplines and their foundations, it is necessary to understand where they come from and how they differ from previous, or competing, idea systems.

Feudalism

The elements of contemporary criminal justice systems in western liberal democracies like Canada and the U.S. were founded in the turmoil of the period of the late seventeenth to early nineteenth centuries, in the collapse of feudalism and the rise of capitalist modernity. These changes transformed class relations and social institutions, and the ideas related to them, in profound ways. Important changes occurred in thinking about relations between society and the state. Notions of contract came to prevail in political matters as they did in economic matters. The social contract in political terms mirrored the economic contract in market terms. Indeed, with the rise of capitalism, the metaphor of the market would come to dominate in all spheres of social life.

Under feudalism, society was divided among three primary estates. These were the serfs, the clergy, and the nobility. These estates were placed on a stratified social hierarchy of privilege. This was a rigidly hierarchical system. If one was born a serf, one would live their entire lives and die as a serf.

Within feudal systems there existed great disparities in wealth and resources within specific populations. Wealth, property, and power were held by the tiny minority of elites, the landed aristocracy or nobility. The clergy were the religious strata who were largely responsible for the realm of ideas.

The vast majority of the population under feudal systems — some 90% — were serfs who existed in conditions of often extreme poverty. These serfs had few "rights" as modern citizens would know them. The tiny ruling portion of the population, the wealthy and privileged nobility, controlled all social wealth and enjoyed the benefits of political and cultural dominance. Law and order resulted from their arbitrary, and often barbarous, decision making.

The administration of justice was unsystematic and very much depended upon the specific interests and motivations of particular local power holders. The justice system was founded in the personal relationships and associations of ruling elites, and positions of authority were distributed on the basis of friendship, family ties, and/or business. Patronage was the order of the day. As well decisions about law, criminality, or punishment were subject to the whim of local elites. Legal authorities held absolute power over life and death and could show mercy or cruelty on the basis of their shifting moods. If a local lord awoke in bad temper, it could prove fatal for an unsuspecting serf accused of some absurd charge such as witchcraft or sorcery.

One might wonder how such a system of gross inequality and injustice could be justified particularly given that the overwhelming majority of the population was deprived of basic economic and political necessities. How might people suffering under such a system have been led to rationalize their suffering? Why did they not refuse to exist under such conditions and rebel against the economic and political elites of the day?

The first part of an answer is that, in fact, they did rebel. The feudal era was marked by a series of peasant rebellions and uprisings. And in response they were brutally tortured and punished. The second, and more complex, answer is that rule was maintained and extended through ideological means. Social inequality was posed as natural, even "god-given." This is where ruling ideas come into play, including ideas about crime and punishment, law and order. Thus, rule consisted of repression and the military suppression of peasant movements. At the same time, rule was underpinned by appeals to tradition and custom.

In the medieval and early modern period as today, elites, largely through the religious caste, the clergy, controlled idea systems and deployed idea systems that justified the ruling order and social hierarchies of the day. Justice was based in an association of the religious functionaries and the landed gentry. The clergy served a function very much similar to contemporary mass media. They were responsible for disseminating ideas about the structure of society and operated as a monopoly. They were the primary purveyors of ideas and, given mass illiteracy, there were few outside their numbers who could read and comment on the primary documents that they produced and relied upon. This gave them even greater powers than today's western mass media who produce and distribute ideas to literate audiences. Furthermore, their access to, and dependence upon, political and economic rulers ensured that their ideas would get the broadest exposure and support — but only if they flattered and supported those political and economic rulers.

The ideas of the medieval clergy, the ideological caste under feudal systems, justified elite rule by the nobility by claiming that the nobles were God's representatives on earth. The nobles were said to be closer to God, even touched by God, and therefore the only earthly beings fit to rule on God's behalf. They were tasked with overseeing the care and maintenance of God's earthly property. This notion is reflected in the so-called "Divine Right of Kings."

One of the key ideological tools deployed by the religious estate to justify rule by nobility was the notion of the Great Chain of Being. The idea of the Great Chain of Being suggested that not all earthly creatures were equally close to God. Instead all creatures, from the lowliest worm through the most powerful royal, were ranked on a ladder of privilege based on their imagined nearness to God. Serfs were less near God than nobles who were said to be touched by God. Serfs were barely human within such a worldview. They were certainly not deemed fit to govern themselves or manage their own affairs. Such responsibilities properly belonged, within this schema, to the nobles, those who, it was claimed, could be relied upon to do God's bidding. Rulership, management of resources, and government were claimed as their divine right. Serfs could make no such claim to any similar rights. The notion of *human* rights made no sense under feudalism since not everyone was equally human. Only the privileged were fully human and could legitimately claim a full range of rights. Serfs and women had few rights.

These references to a mystical entity, a fairy tale, were used opportunistically to justify and reinforce great degrees of human inequality and injustice. In this case, as in others we will examine, the ruling ideas were not the best, most accurate, or most just. They were simply the ideas best suited to maintaining relations of power and domination for the elites who benefited from such social arrangements. Clearly serfs and serf movements offered better understandings of the world based on notions of equality and cooperation and the needs of the vast majority of the population. One can see this by reading the words of reformers and rebels like Gerrard Winstanley. Unfortunately many of these reformers and rebels, like Winstanley himself, were killed by the state precisely because of their ideas. Those alternative ideas did not fit elite interests and so they were not chosen, supported, or circulated through the dominant channels of the day — though they did circulate through conversations in face to face venues among non-elites within communities of the poor and oppressed. They did not become ruling ideas, though they did gain influence as the feudal systems began to collapse and movements of the poor became more expansive and powerful.

The absurdity of ruling ideas can be seen clearly in viewing ideas of crime and punishment within feudal systems. That such ideas ruled people's lives, and contributed to much human misery and suffering, is a testament to the power of elites in selecting and wielding ideas that advance their interests against the needs of the majority of a population.

The Demonic View of Crime and Punishment

Prior to the modern period of liberal democratic politics and capitalist economics — thousands of years through to the collapse of feudalism in the late 1600s in the West — behaviors that might be considered deviant or criminal were attributed to demons, evil spirits, or forces of nature. These ideas were driven largely by religious beliefs and explanations that drew upon and reinforced religious worldviews. There is anthropological indication of some societies attempting to release evil spirits by drilling holes into the skull of the afflicted, a process known as trephination.

While demonic theories do not influence criminal justice system policies today, they are still part of popular media accounts of some sensational crimes. Cases like the Son of Sam murders and the Manson Family killings are portrayed in some media accounts in relation to influences by demonic spirits or Satanism. Some religions, such as Catholicism, still make reference to spirit possession and engage practices of exorcism to force the spirit out of the afflicted person's body. In addition, the belief in spirits and otherworldly beings as factors in human life persists in the present day in countries like Canada and the U.S. For example, various recent studies have found that the majority of people in the U.S. believe in angels and demons (Pew 2007; Baylor 2008). Similar results have been reported in the U.K. (Heathcote-James 2002).

Under medieval and early modern systems crime and deviance were viewed, not solely as harms done to individuals or society, but rather as harms done to God. Crimes were universal in impact. Thus punishment, no matter how minor the crime, should always be severe, since the real impact of crime was an injury to God's order.

Within religion-based feudal worldviews, crime and deviance were attributed to the actions of gods and demons. Within these perspectives people were said to commit crimes either because they were possessed by evil beings, perhaps the devil itself, or they were being punished by God for some transgression. Deviance and crime were viewed as being rooted in the body, or even the soul or spirit of the perpetrator, usually through an invasion by some form of evil being.

Given the hierarchical and authoritarian character of the society, the only ones suited to determine guilt or innocence were the elites, the nobility, or the clergy. The mechanism for determining guilt or innocence was through a trial by ordeal. The accused individual was literally put through a physical ordeal, the outcome of which would determine guilt or innocence — though in reality guilt was predetermined and few could survive the typically barbaric and violent abuse to which they were subjected. Infamous examples include the practice of determining guilt or innocence by tying a rock to someone and throwing them in a lake. If they floated they were possessed by evil and should be punished, or more likely killed. If they sank, well they were innocent but also dead. At least their souls would be set free. Other trials included stretching on racks, boiling in oil, being placed in "iron maidens," cylinders lined with spikes in which the accused was placed. Needless to say, regardless of guilt or innocence, the accused almost always ended up dead.

More than a way to determine guilt or innocence, the trial by ordeal was meant as a show of the total and absolute power and authority of the nobility and clergy who ordered and oversaw the trials by ordeal. It also showed force-fully that non-elites could, at any time and for any reason, be subjected to the will of the political, economic, and cultural elites who viewed themselves as their superiors.

The Rise of Capitalism, the Social Contract, and Classical Criminology

Beginning in England in the seventeenth century, with the English Civil War, and emerging in other countries of Western Europe through the twentieth century, feudal relations collapsed in revolutions and wars. The power and authority of the nobility and the clergy were confronted and broken. As economic structures changed, so too did idea systems.

Over the course of several centuries, one mode of production — feudalism — based on agricultural production, landed wealth, and hereditary authority gave way to another mode of production — capitalism. Capitalist relations emerged on the basis of commercial market economies within specific national boundaries — what is called mercantilism — and developed economies based on industrial power and production relations.

Under the emerging capitalist system, based on market dominance and private productive capital rather than landed wealth, the feudal estates collapsed to be replaced over time by new economic structures and new class relations. Rather than a society organized around three major estates, capitalist socioeconomic arrangements divided society increasingly between two primary classes based on their relationship to ownership and control of productive property such as workplaces and resources. The ruling property owning class of economic elites is known as the bourgeoisie. They represent a tiny, but powerful minority within capitalist societies. The majority of society, those who have nothing to sell except their labour, represent the proletariat — the non-elite working classes.

The emergence of mercantilist capita systems — merchant trading within a national context — pushed against the absolute power of the monarchy that ruled over the local landowners. Whereas feudal lords claimed political rights on the basis of hereditary privilege, the new ruling groups of capitalism, the capitalist class or bourgeoisie, claimed political authority on the basis of market success and private control of productive property.

The fact that monarchs were solely responsible for granting monopoly trading rights to companies of their choosing (like the Hudson's Bay Company or the East India Trading Company) was viewed as an unfair advantage that harmed local merchant capitalists and worked against their economic interests. They resented the monopoly control exercised by the nobility over such economic matters.

A political revolution was necessary to change decision making capacities and shift power and authority to the emergent ruling class of merchant capitalists and away from the landed aristocracy and monarchy. Indeed, the English Revolution, French Revolution, and American Revolution did serve, in varying degrees to limit or replace the power of the monarchy in each context. New political institutions (especially liberal democratic parliaments) were established and the monarchy lost power — along with, for many of them, their heads. More regular and systematic, and less arbitrary and personalized, systems of governance emerged that were more suited to the trading needs of market capitalists who needed reliable prices and trading conditions as expressed in laws that applied equally to all merchants.

With the collapse of feudal systems and the rise of new groups seeking ruling status, new ideas would emerge, including ideas about law and order, crime and punishment. The new ruling class, the bourgeoisie, could not rely on the ruling idea systems that prevailed under feudalism. Their appeals to dominance could no longer be based on claims to be closer to God and on appeals to hereditary rights and authority. The new ruling class had not been among the groups identified as having divine rights and they were not the traditional or hereditary holders of power. Their power came through economic success, not privileged family histories. Thus, they could not rely on the claims to dominance made by the nobility.

At the same time they did not want the faltering nobility to attempt to reclaim their power through appeals to religious favor or hereditary privilege. There was real fear that the nobles would make demands on their previous property on the basis that only they were entitled by family heritage and traditional law. The wealth of the bourgeoisie was based, not on traditional land title, but upon mobile, productive capital and trade. They required a new idea system to justify their rule and they found it in the form of political liberalism — the notion that the state should regulate individual public behavior while protecting private property from intrusion by the community or by the non-property owning working classes. For the new ruling elites, the state should support the rule of the market through laws, police, and the military.

In the late 1600s and early 1700s, as feudal arrangements broke down and the grip of religion as the dominant perspective on life was loosened, new intellectual movements emerged to challenge for prominence and social influence. These periods of intellectual innovation came to be known as the Renaissance, the Age of Reason and the Enlightenment. The intellectual invention of the Enlightenment changed perspectives on various social issues, including crime, law, and punishment. These developments would contribute to the rise of social sciences such as sociology, psychology, and criminology. Notions of political democracy, human rights, and legal equality gained momentum against ideas that had justified hereditary privilege, traditional authority, and rule by a landed aristocracy. Notably the new ideas called for increased participation in political affairs, but only for specific people and groups — those new elites who owned and controlled property.

Among the key concepts to emerge, which would come to dominate social thought in liberal democracies like Britain, Canada, and the U.S., is the notion of a social contract. The political philosopher Thomas Hobbes argued famously in his book *Leviathan* that the "natural state" of human life, in pre-social conditions, was "nasty, brutish, and short." Hobbes, influenced by the turmoil of the period during the English Civil War, argued that humans are by nature self-interested or egoistic and this pursuit of self-interest is the source of all human conflict. In order to avoid conflict, and out of fear of harm from others, humans came to form a social contract with each other resulting in the formation of political states. For Hobbes, the state, though unnatural, a fabrication, provides a protective function and is, therefore, rational. In exchange for protection from the state, people give up their natural rights and restrain their behavior.

In fact, most anthropological history refutes Hobbes' view of non-state societies. Non-state societies, far from being nasty and brutish, tend to be cooperative and peaceful based on mutual aid and solidarity rather than egoism and competition. Most of human history has, in reality, flourished in the absence of states. Anthropologists such as Pierre Clastres show that in tribal societies, whenever a form of state threatens to emerge, the society acts to force out those who would seek to usurp social power and serve as a state in the making.

Hobbes as a political elite provided a distorted view of history and society that served the interests of the emerging post-feudal social order and the interests of new elites within the state. He told the classes of political power holders what they wanted to hear and provided a mechanism for intellectually justifying new relations of rule. No longer was elite rule justified by the chain of being and religious privilege. Under the emerging post-feudal arrangements, appeals to power had to appear in a form palatable to the new classes whose authority was based not on historic claims. The notion of the social contract suggested that the subjected consented to be ruled by elites, without any actual sign of that consent.

Another key figure in social contract theory was the philosopher John Locke. Identified by some as the "father of liberalism," Locke also focused on relationships between the individual and the state. Locke argued against philosophers who suggested that people were born with fully fledged personalities that only needed to grow into maturity. Locke suggested that human personality is like a blank slate at birth — a *tabula rasa* — on which social experience and societal influences write individual personalities. Rather than primary products of nature, humans are largely products of nurture. Locke's work would influence later social constructionist perspectives and sociological works that emphasize the effect of social experience on human development. It has also influenced criminological approaches that argue against notions that criminals are born rather than made. Locke also offered a version of the social contract to explain human collective life within society.

Idea systems do not change simply because new and better ideas come along. They emerge as part of broader economic, social, political, and geographic transformations. It is not coincidence that the rise of a mercantilist, merchant capitalist, class that gained wealth through market exchange should give rise to notions of society organized around social *contracts*. The contract was the relationship of predominance at the market and, for the emergent bourgeoisie, it provided the justification for the reorganization of society and the state on a basis that reflected and reinforced their market preoccupations.

Conflict and the Emergence of Modern Criminology

By the time of the French Revolution of 1789, which dramatically broke up the feudal arrangements in France, starvation, poverty, and destitution were rampant among the vast majority of the population who were working class, peasants, and/or poor. The tiny minority of the population who controlled the resources of society feared the majority of the population who were desperate and angry about their social situation and conditions of life. As the French Revolution showed through the guillotine, the ruling classes of society had much to fear.

Any small group with social, economic, and political privilege that is surrounded by a much larger group that is socially, economically, and politically deprived has reason to be concerned. Despite the liberalization of state practices, democratization of government, and discourses of human rights, the emergent elites of the eighteenth and nineteenth centuries still deployed ruthless force to punish and warn those who threatened their privilege and authority. Social unrest, rebellions, and uprisings were met by legislative as well as military measures. So too were more modest reform movements. Protest leaders and community and workplace organizers continued to be subjected to violence, arrest, detention, torture, and execution.

Laws reinforced the elites' claims on their disproportionate and unjust control of resources. Property laws and laws requiring the poor to labour for elites became paramount. Privilege was the basis for laws and punishments leveled largely against those without privilege.

Within feudal systems, despite the great imbalances in power and wealth, there were limits on power and elites were expected to meet certain obligations to serfs. For example, while peasants were required to turn over a portion of their productive labours (crops, livestock, fuel, and so forth) to the local feudal lord, it was also expected that the lord would provide security for serfs and protection against external threats such as invasion of their lands and villages. As well there were obligations to provide food to serfs in terms of famine or want. This is where the notion of *noblesse oblige* (noble obligations) originates. Peasants also had the right to feud, to appeal for redress of grievances in cases where they may have been wronged.

Notions of social contract and individual rights broke these bonds of obligation between nobility and serfs. Private property, and its defense in laws, also served capital by unilaterally cancelling the claims of serfs to the common lands — the commons — that they relied on for subsistence (food and shelter). Enclosure acts legally turned common lands over to private control by capital and military force violently prohibited serfs from accessing the lands that had traditionally sustained their communities for generations. The state became the new sovereign that ruled social relations on the basis of property and individual rights rather than traditional obligations and collective rights (such as community rights to the land, food, and shelter).

The Enlightenment influenced notions of crime, criminality, and punishment. It contributed to the development of ideas that focus on human rationality and reason in understanding social life, social problems, and criminal behavior. The dominance of religious worldviews and superstitions was challenged.

The new perspectives on crime and punishment are known as classical criminology. They will be more closely examined in the following chapter. Classical criminology set the stage for criminal justice systems that focus on the lower level street crimes of the poor and working classes, while ignoring the high level crimes committed by private interests, such as corporate executives and business leaders. Classical criminology, by overlooking conditions of class, poverty, and inequality, served the interests of the new property owning classes who desired and sought a means for justifying their social privilege in a stratified society in which there was much deprivation for the non-property owning classes.

CHAPTER 3

Non-Sociological Theories: The Rise of Classical Criminology and the Limits of Liberalism

M ost of the popular explanations of crime — and certainly those that dominate both the mass media and the present-day criminal justice systems in liberal democracies like Canada and the U.S. — are non-sociological. That is, these explanations focus largely on the individual — either in terms of rationality or irrationality or in terms of mental causes or psychological attributes or the biological traits of identified offenders. Notably, non-sociological theories — especially classical criminology theories — also dominate criminology as an academic discipline; both historically and in the present day.

This chapter examines non-sociological theories of crime and punishment that continue to influence criminal justice system policy, media accounts and criminological courses and research. It focuses on what is known as classical criminology or the classical school.

Classical Criminology

What might be understood as a criminological perspective emerged in the late eighteenth and early nineteenth centuries. Referred to as the classical school of criminology, this criminological perspective, or range of perspectives, would provide the philosophical and practical underpinnings for modern criminological systems. Indeed the criminal justice systems in contemporary liberal democracies like Canada are still organized according to the principles of classical criminology.

The most influential figure in developing classical criminological perspectives was Cesare Beccaria (1738-1794), a jurist, politician, and author based in Italy. In 1764, Beccaria argued, in his influential work *Essay in Crime and Punishment*, for a system of justice based on human reason rather than on the religious doctrine of "an eye for an eye."

Classical criminology was also greatly influenced by the works of utilitarian philosophers, especially Jeremy Bentham (1748-1832). Utilitarianism expressed the view that reason should dictate that actions are undertaken that secure the greatest good for the greatest number. Utilitarianism is also closely associated with hedonism — the notion that actions are undertaken by rational individuals as they seek to increase pleasure while limiting pain. Bentham also espoused a belief in the social contract — the exchange of some freedoms for the hope of protection — as the basis for social order.

The main proponents of classical criminology opposed the arbitrary nature of decision making about crime as carried out under feudal regimes. Notions of right and wrong, guilt or innocence, should not be dependent on the personal whims of nobles or clergy relying on appeals to superior beings or mystical forces. Classical criminology also opposed the barbaric response to crime and deviance that characterized medieval practices of punishment, including trials by ordeal and torture. Against the arbitrary and barbaric nature of punishment under medieval regimes, classical criminology advocated the rule of law in which all people, regardless of life situation, are treated equally, without fear or favor in dealings with the criminal justice system. Indeed, classical criminology constructs an abstract individual and suggests that all should be treated the same before the law without regard to their experiences or opportunities or to the barriers and obstacles they face in their lives. While this may seem egalitarian, it can, and does, have unequal and unfair consequences in practice.

The response to crime among classical criminologists was related to their understanding of the causes and consequences of crime. For classical theorists like Beccaria, crime was not an injury to God or the universe, but, rather, an injury to society. Punishment should be directed at avoiding further injury to society. As such, punishment should serve primarily, not the desires of vengeance or exorcism, but the function of deterrence, discouraging further crimes.

Classical criminology views people as rational, calculating actors who seek to maximize pleasure and minimize pain. People act with free will, according to their perceived needs. Punishment is best where it works to deter rational calculators from engaging in specific activity by raising the cost — social, physical, or financial — of the action in question. Criminality is not a matter of demonic possession or mystical forces but, rather, an outcome of making the wrong choice or personal calculation. If people are rational calculators, crime is simply an adding mistake. The consequence is punishment.

Punishment should deter rational calculators. For theorists like Beccaria, deterrence occurs at two levels — the specific and the general. It should be directed both at the individual and society at large. Individual deterrence should work to ensure that individuals who engage in criminal activity are discouraged from doing so again after they are caught. This would be achieved through a punishment that outweighs the perceived benefits of committing the crime and which brings some cost or pain to the individual. This pain is not understood as solely as physical pain but might be social pain through public shaming or financial pain through fines or lost income. General deterrence works to discourage people who observe or find out about criminal activity from engaging in such activity themselves. This occurs by observing or learning of the punishment applied to a convicted offender. Punishment should serve to fix the calculation, to remove the margin of error for weighing costs and benefits. Punishment is situated as part of broader social control mechanisms that are developed to help people to decide properly between right and wrong, acceptable and unacceptable behavior.

Society is itself, for classical theorists, an outcome of rational, self-interested calculation. People come together to increase their individual chances for survival and to reduce the effort required to survive. Classical criminologists argue that in order to interact beneficially with other people, individuals enter into a contract with society — a social contract — between individuals and the state. The social contract is a central concept within classical criminology referring to an implied agreement in which individuals give up some rights or freedoms in exchange for protection from the state. This is a market-based view of human nature. It differs from more co-operative views of human nature that argue that society forms through mutual aid and mutual labour and collective decision making rather than individual choices. Classical theorists assume that there exists a social consensus about what is good or bad, right or wrong.

In opposition to the barbaric practices of feudal times, Beccaria argued that punishment should not be excessive. Punishment should be levied in proportion to the harm actually committed — it should be appropriate to the crime. For punishment to serve as an effective deterrent, it should be delivered as near in time to the criminal act as possible. The time between crime and punishment should not be distant or the punishment will have diminished impact. In Beccaria's view, the carrying out of punishment should be certain as well as swift. The accused, as well as general members of society at large, should be well aware of the consequences of specific criminal acts so that they can make the adequate and appropriate calculations about whether or not to engage in any act.

Laws should be clearly written and publicly accessible so that judges have little leeway to interpret it. The task of judges should simply be to decide whether or not the law has been broken.

The Panopticon: Classical Criminology and the Surveillance Society

The idea that punishment should be instructive or serve as a warning to society at large led to a range of proposals from classical criminologists who sought practices and institutions that would encourage or direct people to regulate their activities according to the calculus of hedonistic and utilitarian logic. A key innovation was the panoptic prison, or panopticon, proposed by utilitarian philosopher Jeremy Bentham.

The panopticon was Bentham's plan for a cylindrical prison structure designed such that all prisoners in a ward could be observed at all times by a single guard placed in a tower in the centre of the ward. Significantly, while the guard could view all prisoners and monitor their activities, the prisoners could never see the guard. Thus, they could never know if the guard was present or absent at any given time. Bentham argued that simply the possibility that the guard might be present and observing them, without their knowledge, would cause prisoners to regulate their own behaviors — to self-regulate. Notably, they would do so all the time, even when no one was in the guard tower. The guards, and their regulatory regimes, would, in essence, enter the prisoners' consciousness. The guards would be "in their heads" so to speak. For Bentham, not only would this serve the interests of carceral control and punishment within institutions. Revealing his interests as a defender of the market and private capital, Bentham suggested that the panopticon would also allow for a reduction of labour costs because fewer prison staff would be required. Because prisoners would regulate themselves whether guards were present or not, there did not need to be a guard present within a ward at all times. Thus, Bentham shows the concern of classical criminology with market mechanisms and, ultimately, with control of workers.

Even more, though, Bentham did not only view the panopticon as a mechanism of control within prison. He viewed it as a means of social control more broadly, particularly within working class communities. During the time in which Bentham was writing, the late eighteenth and early nineteenth centuries, working people lived within walking distance of their workplaces. Transit systems as we know them today did not exist and there were no automobiles. As a matter of cost and convenience, people lived near their workplaces and entire neighbourhoods were built near workplaces, particularly factories, simply to house the people who worked in those workplaces. In this context Bentham suggested that panoptic prisons be built within working class communities. That way working people, who might be angry or unsatisfied with their working or living conditions and planning to protest or organize social movements would have a constant, visible reminder of the punishment that would await them should they step out of line. Potential union organizers could look out of the windows of the factory at which they worked and see the prison that would soon house them should they engage in workplace activism or sabotage. Thus, once again, the classical criminologist is seen to be preoccupied with the concerns and interests of the property owning classes rather than the concerns of the toiling masses or the poor who sought better lives and labours.

As a utilitarian, Bentham argued that punishment should be more painful than the benefits accrued from breaking the law. Applying the notion of hedonistic calculus, he suggested that individuals weigh the consequences of their behavior before acting to maximize pleasure or minimize pain. The panopticon would offer a visual reminder of the consequences of acting in unacceptable ways. It would also serve as a threat that behavior would not pass unnoticed.

Social theorist Michel Foucault used Bentham's notion of the panopticon as a useful metaphor for modern disciplinary regimes and growing tendencies within society to observe and regulate ourselves and others. One might think about the panopticon in relation to the surveillance of public spaces in the twenty-first century. The development and widespread placement of surveillance cameras and security systems might represent contemporary forms of panoptic observance. Some might suggest that in the twenty-first century, countries like Canada and the U.S. represent panoptic societies in which everyone is watching everyone else through means that are not immediately visible, such as cell phone cameras or private security systems. Surveillance is seemingly ever present, whether within workplaces as bosses keep watch over workers or in open public spaces at intersections or town squares. Even the capacity to monitor the computer activity of others means that the panopticon operates within our most intimate spaces within our own homes monitoring our interests, wishes, and desires. You might ask yourself how much you regulate or restrain your own behavior as a result of perceptions about the prevalence of surveillance.

Legacies of the Classical School of Criminology

The classical school of criminology made several important contributions to theories and practices of criminal justice. It certainly moved thinking about crime and punishment in some progressive directions away from the arbitrary and barbarous practices of medieval systems. There are several lasting advances made by the classical school.

First is the emphasis on rationality and human will. The classical school made central to its perspective the idea that people act on the basis of consideration and choice. They moved the emphasis away from demons, possessions, spirits, and otherworldly forces as factors in human action. They emphasized that people could make the world rather than being passive subjects. They also recognized that people take responsibility for their actions.

Second, they shifted the emphasis on punishment from retribution and revenge to deterrence and rehabilitation. Crimes are harms to individuals and society, rather than offenses against God or the universe. The proper response to crime is to encourage people, those engaged in crime and those witnessing it, to act differently, to alter their behavior in a way that does not impose harm. Revenge serves no greater purpose, either to the individuals involved or to society more broadly. An eye for an eye leaves everyone blind, as the saying goes. Thus, classical criminology, while not eliminating barbaric or violent practices from criminal justice systems entirely, did help to reduce levels of barbarism while removing many egregious practices.

Third, classical criminology moved the focus of criminal justice onto the act committed and away from the person committing it. The emphasis came to be placed on the act and its associated harms rather than identifying an individual as fundamentally flawed or "possessed" by evil. For classical criminology, all people are viewed as potentially capable of good or capable of bad. Appropriate responses, in terms of punishment, should make the choice to do good deeds more likely than the choice to do bad ones. In addition, it has to be shown that the act in question is a real problem. One should not be punished simply according to unjustified claims or on the basis of an arbitrary judgment, impulse, or whim of some authority. No one should be thrown in a lake or tied to a rack simply because a privileged member of society desires it.

Finally, and perhaps most significantly, classical criminology emphasized individual rights and due process within criminal justice systems. Society owes people respect and must recognize their liberty. The accused are to be presumed innocent until proven otherwise, within processes that are open and consistently applied. Classical criminology encouraged more open and systematic approaches to justice. It argued for important restrictions on judicial discretion.

Significantly, classical criminology recognized that society has a duty and obligation to the individual as much as the individual has any duty or obligation to society. Individuals should expect certain conditions of life within the society in which they live and have, as unique individuals, fundamental freedoms and liberties that must be respected by others, including by authorities. Even more, if society, and particularly the state, is not meeting its duties and obligations or respecting people's liberties and freedoms, people are right to rebel and seek new arrangements. People maintain a fundamental and unalienable right to rebel.

Limitations of Classical Criminology

While classical criminology made some important contributions to thinking about criminality and justice, moving beyond the arbitrary and barbaric approaches of medieval practices, it has a number of limitations. These limitations are related to the lack of social vision and analysis — the lack of sociological imagination — within classical theories.

First, general principles do not always serve the interests of justice. Treating people the same, without regard to social context, may provide abstract "equality" before the law but not real equality or justice. Notions of "equality before the law" mask often massive social inequalities in the real world. People do not have the same choices or opportunities available to them. People may, in fact, offend solely because of social inequalities. Someone who is homeless may break into and squat in an abandoned building, not because they are irrational, but because they need shelter and have no other available options.

Second, who gets to decide what is rational? If you are homeless and need shelter, is it rational to stay outside and freeze to death or is it rational to break into an abandoned building and squat for the night? If you are hungry, is it rational to starve or to steal food? The law is not about rationality. It is about privileging specific interests, typically those of property, over others, even where needs would suggest the absence of laws. Thus, in liberal democracies like Canada and the U.S., the law privileges property owners who hold buildings empty to speculate on land sales and profits over the life and death needs of homeless people.

Furthermore, people are not equally rational and/or do not have equal access to information or opportunities that would allow for the most beneficial choices to be made in specific circumstances. Many factors can influence reason or rationality.

Similarly, laws that are applied equally may never impact the wealthy and may only ever, in reality, be deployed against the poor. The Safe Streets Act in British Columbia applies to rich and poor alike but, obviously, only the poor need to panhandle or squeegee wash car windshields to survive. The real question must ask why criminal justice systems in liberal democracies like Canada put more resources into laws that overwhelmingly capture the poor rather than laws that involve activities primarily undertaken by the wealthy, such as corporate safety.

Classical criminology fails to address either the substantive causes of social inequality or the underlying power imbalances in society that give rise to crime and deviance in the first place. The limited nature of contemporary criminal justice systems in democratic polities like Canada and the U.S. is very much related to the origin of those systems in the liberal political thought of classical criminology and utilitarian philosophy. Classical liberal philosophers, critical of the unitary and totalitarian worldview of feudalism, argue that freedom and liberty must be understood in individualistic terms. For liberal theorists, each individual is said to possess a sphere of personal autonomy that allows the individual to pursue its own self interests.

The classical theorists argue for a separation of private and public realms. Ensuring that individuals could enjoy personal freedoms is understood primarily in commercial or market terms. Issues of personal freedom are constructed as market relations and private property "rights." Classical liberalism argues that these are properly left to a private sphere that is beyond community regulation. Rights, within such perspectives, mean protecting the supposedly private realms of property and markets against possible intrusion, or regulation, by the community. The state is understood as a threat to freedom — particularly the private freedoms of commerce. The state, within liberal philosophy, is accorded a limited sphere of action — particularly the functions of collective force represented by policing, national defense and militarism, and colonial expansion and the expansion of markets beyond national borders. Thus, the privileging of property, and the overwhelming focus on crimes against property, within criminal justice systems in modern liberal democracies prevail.

Legal structures in western democracies are underpinned by the same principles of liberalism that are used to justify the market economy and representative, rather than participatory, democratic political institutions. This represents a "legal liberalism" in which laws, policing, and courts support the market economy, protect private property, and reinforce an individualistic conception of rights in which rights are viewed as possessions of an individual rather than collectives. Rights are understood as guards against intrusion by the community but not as guards against intrusion by the market or private capital. This helps to explain why the rights of property owners to keep residences empty despite mass homelessness are held above and beyond the rights of homeless people to squat in those empty buildings, even if it is a matter of life and death. While making useful contributions to reforming justice systems, it does not provide a basis for more fundamental change.

The Social Context of Classical Criminology

The period during which Beccaria and Bentham and the other classical criminologists wrote was a time of economic turmoil, wars, and revolutions. It was a period marked by the violent collapse of the feudal estates and noble rule, and the rise of capitalist social relations and rule by the bourgeoisie or merchant class of property owners. It was also a period in which the poor, the serf communities, lost access to the common lands that sustained them and during which they mobilized to demand greater say in political affairs and more power within the newly emerging society.

The notion of humans as rational calculating actors pursuing their own selfish interests shows the economic roots, and biases, of classical criminology. This is a model of human nature based on a market model of behavior — one that reflects its origins in a market economy — which justifies and rewards preferred behaviors of the market. Beccaria and Bentham — as members of the new bourgeois class — offered analyses that reflected their own interests, and those of their colleagues, and, more broadly, their class in its search for hegemony.

The appeal to individual rights rather than collective or community rights privileged private property over community needs — such as common lands, "the commons." Private property trumped collective or communal claims on resources. Thus, individual rights served an important function for the economic and social aims of the bourgeoisie. The assertion of individual rights justified private capital's control of what had been, and were, public resources — the commons. It provided a legal basis for enclosures of public lands and the mass displacement of peasants from their traditional common lands.

Private property owners, unlike feudal lords, then owed no traditional or customary obligations to others. While control of land under feudalism had been connected with specific obligations — for security, food, and so forth — to those who lived and worked upon the land, notions of private property placed no requirements on the owners of capital. The bourgeoisie or capitalists could dispose of what were now viewed as their personal possessions as they saw fit — no matter the harm or deprivation caused to others.

Lacking collective rights to the land, peasants could be and were dispossessed and displaced. Property laws provided a legal cover for often violent processes of expulsion. Driven from their communal lands, the now landless peasants migrated to the cities where they were forced to survive by selling their labour — the only property they now possessed — to the bourgeoisie. Individual workers lacked property, housing, and food, and could only claim pay for subsistence — if they worked for capital. This process writ large would provide the basis for the expansion and growth of industrial capitalism and factory production in urban centres. Some of these issues, and their impact on criminological theory, are addressed in the next chapter.

CHAPTER 4

Positivist Criminology: Social Science or Social Control?

T his chapter looks at the influence of the Industrial Revolution on positivist theories of crime in the late nineteenth and early twentieth centuries. Positivist theories claimed to bring the scientific method that drove industrial development to bear on understandings of crime and recommendations for criminal justice system practice. There the pressures of industrialization gave rise to approaches in which science was appropriated and misappropriated by criminologists looking to establish themselves as professional scientific experts.

Positivism seeks to explain crime primarily by reference to individual differences between people — particularly in terms of biological or psychological characteristics. The factors that mark people as different are said to predispose some people to crime more than others. Dealing with crime is said to involve identifying and targeting these factors and/or the individuals who might exhibit them. Thus, positivism once again represents approaches that individualize social problems, crime, and punishment. Causes and solutions are sought deeply within the fabric of the human body or mind rather than within the fabric of society. Once more, theoretical approaches that claim to be neutral or even value-free can be seen to be rooted within specific historical social relationships and the interests of specific groups within society.

Positivist theories have influenced, and continue to influence various approaches to understandings of crime, deviance, and punishment. Far from being relics of the past, positivist theories influence criminological research and study right up to the present. They also influence criminal justice system practices, though not to the same extent as classical theories.

Relations of Production: Positivism, Industrialism, and Social Conflict

By the late nineteenth and early twentieth centuries, the rapid growth and expansion of capitalist social relations gave rise to new modes of organizing society. Industrial production in the nineteenth century fully supplanted agricultural and merchant trading, and mercantilism, as the dominant productive arrangement and means of extracting profit from labour. Steam engines provided transformative means of mass production. Railways offered new means for mass exchange and greatly increased access to resources and expanded the range exchange. Both steam engines and railways served as time saving devices and allowed for reductions in labour costs.

In particular, the Industrial Revolution and the reliance on mechanized workplaces as central to capitalist production placed greater emphasis on the applications of science and scientific innovation to economic development. Science became a motive force in industry as competitive markets drove pursuit of new materials, procedures, and products. The Industrial Revolution showed the significant outcomes that could result from the use of scientific method wedded to industrial efficiency, and driven by competitive desires. Once again, the motivations and interests of economic forces would come to influence, shape, and drive intellectual production.

The shifting socioeconomic environment gave rise to new modes of producing knowledge and new systems for describing social relations and human behavior. A period of moral upheaval, associated with the collapse of systems based landed wealth and hereditary claims to resources and the emergent dominance of merchant capital, gave rise to classical theories of justice. A period of scientific expansion of industry, and systems based on productive capital, gave rise to industrial and scientific knowledge claims.

As scientific approaches and applications became central to industrial production, and scientists found lucrative rewards for their labours, new pressures and inducements arose for intellectual workers, particularly researchers in university settings. More and more the scientific method spread to academic disciplines beyond the hard sciences in which it originated. Particularly, the new academic disciplines that sought to establish themselves in the early twentieth century — notably, sociology and psychology — turned to the scientific method as a means of gathering information or data, but also, as importantly as a way to gain credibility and justify the activities of the discipline as being sufficiently academic. Thus, quantitative research methods and the reliance upon statistics would come to be central features of disciplines such as sociology, geography, and especially psychology. This was a period of new professions in the "human sciences" and the growing authority of "experts" who achieved status on the basis of "scientific" approaches to addressing and "solving" social problems. The knowledge claims of these competing experts meshed nicely with the desires of newly established elites to regulate and control working class and poor populations and more effectively extract profit from their labours.

The discipline of criminology, itself struggling to distinguish itself from its senior disciplines of sociology and psychology, was no different in this regard. Criminologists of the early twentieth century, seeking to establish themselves as respected, and valued, experts, took up scientific methods and approaches to research. They made claims to scientific rigor as means to gain credibility and to catch the attention of governments seeking solutions to emerging and worsening social problems. Positivist social scientists asserted that the methods used to study physical matters, such as chemistry or biology, could adequately be used to study social relations. For positivists, science could use data on the social world to prove the existence of causal relationships between crime and specific human traits. The positivist researchers rejected the humanism of the classical school, refusing to accept philosophical or moral definitions of human action. Instead they argued for the necessity of raw data evaluated by social researchers, social "scientists," who were supposedly value-neutral or value-free. As we will soon see, however, claims of value neutrality often masked, or excused, research that was highly motivated by political and economic concerns, particularly the needs of elites in society.

The growth of industrial production was associated with other key transformations in the making of capitalist modernity. At the same time as industries grew, urbanization expanded working class populations in factory towns and cities. With the enclosure of common lands and the spread of private property regimes, the majority of the population in countries like England shifted from being communally organized peasants working the land, to industrial proletarians, the working classes, working in industrial workshops in the growing industrial centres like Manchester and Birmingham.

New forms of struggle emerged along with new claims on justice and threats to privatized ownership of collective resources and productive wealth. Workers and owners, as today, were in day-to-day conflict in workplaces, particularly the new industrial factories. This was different from the occasional battles between peasants and absentee or distant landlords. Even more, the impoverished working class vastly outnumbered the wealthy bourgeoisie in the cities and had easier access to the owners and the property they claimed given the proximity of one to the other in the urban, as opposed to rural, settings.

Labour unions and associations of workers emerged as working people demanded better and safer working conditions. Likewise social reformers sought to improve life for people in the poor and crowded industrial slums. Community movements called for the redistribution of wealth in society. Some labour unions and workers' organizations sought a complete reorganization of production and called for workplaces to be the property of the workers who laboured within them — the call for workers' control of productive property.

Elites continued, as under feudalism and early modernity, to fear rebellion by subjected classes and pursued means for regulating and restricting the activities of non-elites. The bourgeois class of property owners sought, as they do today, to control the working classes through laws and force together. Thus, the modern police forces emerged to act as standing armies to regulate labour and the poor, and ensure that they obeyed the dictates of state and capital and accepted the unequal social hierarchy and their place within it. There will be more on these matters in a later chapter. Unions were outlawed despite the stated claims of liberal politicians and policy makers to respect for freedom of (business) association.

Not only did elites pursue the more established mechanisms of control through law and force; they also turned to the emerging experts and professionals and their new "human sciences" to devise means of control through identification, classification, and surveillance. Moral regulation and the instruction of the working classes in the proper attitudes and behavior desired by the ruling elites also became an important part of these new practices of governance. Those who opposed capital, spoke out against injustice, or refused to accept their living or working conditions were labelled as anti-social, deviant, or pathological, and subjected to criminal punishment or psychological — or "moral" — therapy.

Science in the Service of Inequality: Social Darwinism and Survival for the Fittest

The pursuit of social control mechanisms gave rise to new ways of thinking about human society, crime, deviance, and justice. Positivist approaches become central to social thought as the social sciences gain ground in academic and public discourse. The new hybrids of social thought and science would very easily lend themselves to explanations of social life and development that justified inequality and exploitation.

One of the great influences on positivist criminology, as on scientific thinking more broadly, was provided by the biological works of Charles Darwin (1809-1882). Darwin's general theory of evolution changed thinking about natural — and social — development. For Darwin, traits suited to species survival within natural environments are selected over generations through reproductive processes. Those traits that were most suited to *species* survival in *specific* environments are passed on genetically within species.

Notably, social "science" became wedded to political and social motivations and policies preferred by dominant classes. The early sociologist, Herbert Spencer (1820-1903), one of the founding figures in academic sociology, appropriated, erroneously, Darwin's notion of natural selection in biology and misapplied it to explain human societies and social development. It was, in fact, Spencer, not Darwin, who devised the term "survival of the fittest." How does one measure fitness in human societies? For the Social Darwinists, the answer was clear — wealth. Wealth was viewed as an outcome of biological or social fitness. Spencer used this misappropriation of science to argue that the poor and destitute were biologically inferior. Thus, poverty was explained not by reference to economic issues — unemployment rates, job markets, social distribution of wealth, land ownership — or to political issues — trade legislation, corporate taxation, migration policies, housing, or education — but rather to supposed biological causes present at birth. The notion of survival of the fittest applied to human societies is a politically motivated excuse and justification for inequality and exploitation disguised as "science."

Social Darwinists misused, abused really, Darwin's ideas, making inappropriate and inaccurate references to human societies. They shifted emphasis from species development in natural environments to focus on supposed "fitness" of specific individuals. They also ignored the particular environmental contexts that were so important to Darwin himself.

Using the notion of survival of the fittest, Spencer and the Social Darwinists argued that the poor should be left to die of starvation or ill health and no public money should be spent to support them or improve their conditions of life. To do so, according to the Social Darwinists, would be to take money from the "fittest" in society (the wealthy) and give it to the unfit. That would not only be a waste of resources, it would ensure that the genes of the "least fit" were allowed to reproduce rather than being selected against as nature intended. The implications of such arguments are clearly troubling. The manifestation of Social Darwinist policies in practices of genocide will be discussed later in this chapter.

The poor should be the primary targets of criminal justice policies, laws, policing, and punishment. The aims of criminal justice systems should be not only to protect the property of the economic elites, which should be their first business, but should be to restrain the working classes and poor (the unfit) so that they do not inhibit or impede the activities of the socially fit (the wealthy). The unfit must be kept from interfering with the resources of the fit. Criminal justice systems should reinforce the "natural" selection of the characteristics associated with elites and contribute to survival of the fittest. Of course, there is little that is natural about such processes. Selection in such cases is entirely socially constructed.

Fitness does not predict wealth so much as wealth predicts fitness. A wealthy person might be incompetent and entirely unfit but still be privileged due to family fortune or access to resources. Poor workers might work harder and be more skilled than the idle wealthy but still remain poor. In addition, poverty is well established to be the major contributor to and predictor of health, particularly in times or places where the poor do not have access to affordable health care, as in the period in which Social Darwinism emerged. These are social and economic outcomes not matters of fitness, a term that is ill-defined anyway.

Who is more fit — one who works hard and produces or one who lives off of the labours of their employees? Why measure fitness in material terms? What about people who are poor but well loved by many and respected in their communities compared with wealthy people who are despised and viewed negatively? The notion of fitness is never adequately defined by Social Darwinists, except in a circular manner in which wealth is equated with fitness. The crucial fact is that for humans personal traits are less important than social contexts. Humans have always relied on social units and collective labours to survive. The same traits, in the same individual, can be perfectly adequate for survival — or not — depending on social context.

Exploitation, at home and abroad, became viewed as a natural right of economic and political elites. Power holders explained it as the result of innovations in science and technology. Technological developments were compared with evolution within notions of social evolution. Elites were credited with technological and social progress rather than the intellectual and manual workers who developed and used the technology.

European economic expansion globally expanded Social Darwinist explanations to justify colonial expansion and domination of non-European societies and people. Colonialism and imperialism in Asia, Africa, the Caribbean, South America, and North America, along with the expropriation of lands and labour from indigenous populations, were justified on the basis of European evolution, socially, technologically, and culturally. Europe was said to be socially and biologically more fit and further evolved. The "divine right" of the monarchs became the "evolutionary right" of capital. Science and the expansion of technology in industry provided tools for the conquest of peoples and lands near and far. They also provided justification for practices of domination and control that accompanied conquest.

Among these techniques of domination was the development of racialized categories that classified and ranked people on a hierarchy of development or status. Nineteenth century scientific attempts to classify people gave rise to unscientific categories of race and efforts to catalogue racial types. These categories and the attempts at classification were based not on biological evidence but on social assumptions. Anthropological evidence shows that humans are not divided into different "races." Notions of race, signifying distinct biological categories, have no basis in biology. Rather racial categories are historically and culturally rooted, varying from society to society and over periods of time. In many cultures, and for most of human history, no such categories are used. Notions of race are outcomes of social processes of power that frame how people are viewed on the basis of superficial characteristics. Notably the categories, and how the hierarchies used to rank them, have reflected the biases of predominantly white European scientists who created the categories in the first place and assumed the superiority of people who resembled themselves. Such is a tendency that can be noted throughout various positivist approaches that have influenced thinking about crime and punishment.

These racialized attempts to explain behavior are not, unfortunately, relics of a less enlightened past. They remain active today. A contemporary account that tries to connect racialized categories with crime is offered by the psychologist Phillip Rushton of the University of Western Ontario, in London, Ontario, Canada. In a series of research carried out over years and represented by the book *Race, Evolution and Behaviour* (1995), Rushton argues that black people are more prone to violence and crime. Asians are said to be less violent and more intelligent. White people are located somewhere between the other two classifications. Rushton uses IQ which is well established to be an inaccurate and inadequate, culturally-biased, measure of intelligence. Again, Rushton accepts as natural — race — what is actually a social construction, a fiction even. There is no biological basis for the existence of different races in the human species. Furthermore, crime and violence vary as much within each category as between them. Thus, the supposed differences are not explanatory. Rushton's explanations have no basis in fact. Rather, as for other such research, they reflect existing social stereotypes and structures of inequality within contemporary societies.

Biological Positivism: Neither Social nor Scientific

In criminology, positivist approaches became dominated by what is called biological positivism, or the search for causes of crime within the makeup of human individuals, their bodies, and minds. The works of positivist criminologists harkened back to the demonic approaches to criminality of the medieval period. For positivists, as for the medieval ideologues, the criminal was a distinct character unique from the rest of humanity. Once again, criminals were viewed as born and not made. This was a rejection of the rationalist, liberal humanist approach of classical criminology. In addition, biological positivists suggested that crime and deviance, like other human behaviors, are beyond the direction or control of the person. They are, rather than acting according to reason, acting out deep seated bodily drives. These forces are not the demons or spirits of the medieval systems. They are, rather, physical or biological forces operating within the individual — whether, chemical, mechanical, or genetic.

It is within this context that one must understand the curious theories of Cesare Lombroso, a medical doctor working in Italy in the late nineteenth and early twentieth centuries. At the heart of Lombroso's theory of criminality is the notion of atavism. For Lombroso, criminals are distinct beings — not quite the same biologically as other human beings. Atavists are freaks of nature, evolutionary throwbacks that are not as fully evolved as regular Homo sapiens. They have grown closer to apes than human beings. Atavists are something of a missing link, an anachronism that has grown alongside but distinct from humans — but within human societies. Lombroso lays out the primary characteristics of the atavist in his influential book *On Criminal Man* (1876).

The suggestion that these evolutionary throwbacks or mistakes lived and worked among human societies — and interacted with humans — was cause for much concern for those who accepted the theory. One's neighbour or co-worker, or romantic partner, might be an atavist and they would not even know it. Here Lombroso offers the resolution that would ensure his services were sought after and highly valued. He would guarantee an audience with concerned politicians and civic authorities. This would be done by making the claim that only a highly trained expert, trained in the scientific method and capable of analyzing data — someone very much like himself — possessed the scientific tools necessary to identify and root out the atavists. The positivist criminologist, the one who could diagnose atavism, was worthy of being consulted, and being highly paid for the consultation, on matters of crime and deviance. This is Lombroso's ploy.

Only the trained person of science, the positivist criminologist, could recognize the atavist according to a range of signals that the expert had identified through years of dedicated study. Happily, for society, the biological positivists had identified a variety of physical characteristics that revealed the atavist. Lombroso called these imagined defining characteristics stigmata. Among the distinct features that marked the atavist, Lombroso identified things such as the size of the ears, the shape of the hands, and the angle of the forehead.

Lombroso collected data on the bodily characteristics of numbers of people and attempted to delineate those characteristics that were supposed to be associated with criminality and deviance. Notably, he compared the physical features of people detained in prisons with soldiers in the Italian army. Lombroso identified what he claimed to be significant differences in the appearances of atavistic characteristics between members of the two groups. His work suggests that the imprisoned group is more likely to have rough hands, bumps on the head, sunken eyes, and so on. Thus, for Lombroso, those in prisons — people already identified as criminals — had to be atavists. This is a fine piece of circular reason. People in prison must be atavists and criminals. How do we know this? Well, they are in prison and, therefore, must be criminals.

The dubious, and unscientific, nature of Lombroso's work is signaled by the fact that among the biological markers of the atavist, he includes tattoos. Clearly this is a problem given that people are not born with tattoos — they are not hereditary or naturally occurring. They are culturally defined and determined.

Not only did Lombroso's theories exhibit a class bias against working class males, he also exhibited a patriarchal approach to women expressing what today would be identified as sexist perspectives. Lombroso and Guglielmo Ferrero published biological positivist analyses of women offenders in their book *The Female Offender* (1895). The book was perhaps tellingly subtitled *The Prostitute and the Normal Woman*, revealing the biases it contained. Interestingly, the book proved very popular and was published in English translation even before the now more famous *Criminal Man*. They explained the lower incidence of crime committed by women by suggesting that women had to overcome more self-restraints imposed by the "natural" instincts, such as timidity, supposedly motivating "normal" women. Women had many defects but did not commit as many crimes because of piety, maternity, passivity, and sexual coldness. Deception was among the characteristics said to be held by women that were absent in men but which would prove particularly useful to women engaging in crime. Women who committed crimes were said to be "super males," who combine the criminal features of men with what are supposedly, for Lombroso, the worst features of women. At the same time those women who did engage in criminal activity were said to be more wicked than any men because they had to overcome many obstacles and inhibitions to come to the point of engaging in crime. These atavistic women were also said to be biologically more like men. Lombroso suggests that women who are shorter, with dark hair, and more masculine faces are more likely to commit crime.

Thus, the explanations offered by biological positivists were neither social nor scientific in character. Rather, they were politically charged and reflected and reinforced existing social hierarchies and inequality. The characteristics that Lombroso and his colleagues identified — rough hands, skin bumps, contusions, sunken eyes — were actually characteristics more likely to be associated with manual labour and/or poor nutritional intake. They were measures of class — of working class and poor lives and labour.

Even more, the absurdity of Lombroso's measures is revealed in his inclusion of tattoos among the characteristics that marked an atavist. Clearly tattoos are not biological. They do not appear as part of one's natural physiognomy from birth. As well, it is notable to remember that in the time and place in which Lombroso studied tattoos, far from being widespread as they are today, were more predominant among working class people within specific jobs. Tattoos were, once again markers not of criminality but of class or cultural position.

Overall, Lombroso's methods were entirely flawed. The differences he identified between inmates and military personnel could have been caused simply by chance or by specific policing or military recruitment practices. In the end, the bodily characteristics he observed in inmates might have resulted from poor nutrition and lack of proper hygiene in prison. They might have resulted from or related to prison labour. Beyond this, it is also entirely possible that the characteristics identified by Lombroso as signaling atavism only made certain people more likely to be caught, because their appearance was more memorable, or found guilty, because they looked the part.

Genetic research has ruled out the existence of atavists. There is no evolutionary split, no evolutionary throwback that walks among humans but is not actually human. Despite this, researchers have continued to search for distinguishing factors that mark criminals as different from the rest of humanity. Much of this effort has been disastrous as the next section outlines. The work of such researchers distracts from the important task of understanding social relations in which crime develops and is defined.

Eugenics and Nazi Science: The Underside of Biological Positivism

Biological positivism, and the attempt to locate biological origins of human imperfection or social problems, became something of an obsession for certain scientists and pseudo scientists in North America and Europe. The pursuit of biological answers to social issues would give rise to a range of deeply troubling, even murderous, endeavors in the early and mid twentieth century. Most notably, and infamously, biological positivism contributed to the development of eugenics movements that sought to modify and direct human populations through selective breeding and supposed genetic manipulation. The most horrifying manifestation of eugenics emerged in the Nazi programs of human experimentation and their attempts to exterminate entire populations, including Jewish people and Roma people. The Holocaust, the mass extermination through industrial means, is a direct outcome of the mix of eugenics and industrial capitalism.

Eugenics did not only give rise to horrifying social policies in the countries under Nazi occupation. In Canada, the provincial governments in Alberta under William Aberhart and Ernest Manning, father of Reform Party founder Preston Manning, carried out eugenics-based programs in dealing with people believed to suffer mental illness. In 1928, legislation was passed in Alberta that empowered the government to carry out involuntary sterilization of people classed as "mentally deficient." The Sexual Sterilization Act of 1928 was explicitly directed to deal with "crime, prostitution, and unemployment." These social problems were attributed to personal failing — identified incredibly as "feeblemindedness" — rather than economic factors of poverty, lack of jobs, or labour markets that excluded women. That unemployment is lumped with crime shows, again, that class basis of the legislation. To carry out the programs of detention and sterilization, a four-person Alberta Eugenics Board was formed.

Under successive governments people identified, often wrongly, as being mentally ill were subjected to institutionalization and forced sterilization. Hardly a manifestation of a less informed past, the program was maintained through 1972. During its period of operation, the program approved approximately 5,000 individual sterilizations, carrying out surgeries on 2,832 individuals over 43 years.

Biological Positivism after Eugenics

With the revelations of Nazi atrocities following the end of World War II, eugenics and biological positivism fell out of favor within academic disciplines like criminology for several years. Such research came to be viewed with suspicion. By the 1950s, however, biological positivism made a strong comeback. In criminology, the return of positivism was forcefully expressed in the work of William Sheldon. Sheldon's work would become highly influential, becoming, for a time, one of the dominant theories in criminology.

Sheldon proposed a typology of human body types that he claimed were associated with distinct personalities and dispositions. Body type signals personality type for Sheldon. Sheldon claimed that there are three primary human body shapes — the ectomorph, the endomorph, and the mesomorph. Individuals of different body types are not equally predisposed to criminality. The ectomorph has a slender and weak body type. Sheldon associates this type with an introverted personality. This shy, fragile character is not associated with crime for Sheldon. The endomorph has a round, soft body. Sheldon characterizes the personality of the endomorph as being comfort loving, friendly, and lazy. They are not likely to commit crime in Sheldon's view. The mesomorph is, as the only remaining category, the apparent criminal type. These individuals are hard bodied, muscular, and strong. Their personality is said to be outgoing and aggressive. They are what would more recently be called an alpha. Notably the descriptions offered by Sheldon are simply tired caricatures. The scrawny person is said to be a shy bookworm. The larger, softer body type is portrayed as gregarious and fun loving. The well built person is a tough guy. These are stereotypes more than anything.

Incredibly, Sheldon suggests, against all scientific evidence, that criminal body types result from "bad blood" — a "germ plasma." This already questionable theory then enters into the realm of science fiction rather than science.

Sheldon's theory represents Lombroso's leftovers in a new wrapping with the mesomorph in the role of the atavist. Once more criminals are said to be born and not made. As in Lombroso's theory of atavism, Sheldon's claims fall apart on the slightest scrutiny.

Once again Sheldon accepts the state definitions of crime and focused exclusively on inmates for his supposed criminal population. Almost all of his criminal subjects were working class males who had been convicted for low-level street crimes. The characteristics of the mesomorph may simply be those, again, associated with manual labour. Perhaps people developed mesomorphic body types after being in prison. What if someone is an ectomorph or endomorph at the time they commit the crime, but are a mesomorph at the time of the study because they have been working out while in prison with little else to do? It is also possible, as some have suggested, that deviant subcultures are more likely to recruit stronger, faster, more aggressive members rather than those who are weak, slow, or shy. Thus, rather than the body choosing the crime, the crime chose the body.

Related to this is what happens to the research if white collar and elite criminals are included in the study. Do elite criminals have mesomorphic body types? Does Conrad Black? Dick Cheney? Bernie Madoff? The overwhelming evidence from recent CEOs convicted of crimes suggests otherwise. Of course, Sheldon's theories could not explain this because he accepted elite definitions of crime as activities of the working class and poor and excluded corporate criminals in his research.

Biological positivism, despite the clear problems, and even outright nonsense, associated with much of the research has not gone away. Examples of it recur frequently, continuing in the current century. In the 1960s and 1970s, new forms of biological positivism tried to make connections between criminal activity and individuals with the variation of an extra Y chromosome. Males typically exhibit an XY chromosomal structure while women exhibit an XX structure. Researchers argued for the presence of an extra Y chromosome in some males (XYY) which was said to cause abnormally aggressive behavior in those males. These men are "super males," prone to criminal violence who supposedly show up disproportionately in prison populations.

Once again, however, closer analysis showed serious flaws in the theory. First, despite the appearance of XYY males in prison, 95% of incarcerated males have an XY chromosomal composition (O'Grady 2007). Second, studies have shown that if XYY males end up in prison, it is because of lower socioeconomic status, educational achievement, and performance of those males which relate to higher risks of being caught (O'Grady 2007). Even more, despite the claims that XYY males are more aggressive and violent, research shows that the "super males" are correlated only with property crimes, which are the most criminalized activities in capitalist societies, not crimes of personal violence (O'Grady 2007). Again, these theories serve to shift attention toward individuals who are more likely to be criminalized because of their status rather than raising questions about the why some activities and people of specific backgrounds are more likely to be policed and punished more than others. They shift focus onto the individual and away from the characteristics of social structures and institutions.

Still biological positivism goes on. A recent study published in the journal, *Proceedings of the Royal Society B: Biological Sciences* (Carré and McCormick 2008), argues that facial characteristics are linked to aggressive behavior. The study's authors, Justin Carré and Cheryl McCormick, look at university level hockey players, measuring the width and length of their faces. The researchers conclude that players whose faces appear wider are more aggressive. Aggression in that case is measured on the basis of the number of penalty minutes the players received. In a follow up study in *Psychological Science* (Carré, McCormick, and Mondloch 2009), the researchers suggest that people can assess another person's propensity for violence and aggression simply by looking briefly at a photo of them.

As was true for the classical theories of criminology, positivist criminology is, despite its claims to scientific objectivity, a result of specific social interests related to power, authority, and privilege within a specific, in this case industrial capitalist, society. It echoes and mirrors the viewpoints of economic and political elites and shifts the blame for crime onto the individual — almost exclusively working class male individuals — and away from structures and relations of power, inequality, and exploitation.

Limitations of Positivist Criminology

There are many apparent problems with theories of biological positivism. These problems relate largely to the acceptance of statist definitions of crime and deviance by positivists as well as their misuse of scientific claims and mistaken interpretations of data. Taken together, these problems point to the political nature of biological positivism and reveal the extent to which positivist theories support and reinforce elite interests and concerns. Indeed, positivist theories express elite biases through a language that attempts to hide those biases while claiming scientific foundations for what are, first and foremost, social and political arguments.

First, the biological positivists accept the state's definition of crime and deviance. They focus on people who have been arrested for specific acts and brought within the criminal justice system. Yet they do not include within their analysis those who have committed harmful acts, like pollution or exploitation, but whose activities have not been criminalized or who have not been subject to state surveillance. Typically, elite crimes are less visible because they occur in private settings that police cannot access and are therefore less likely to lead to criminalization for perpetrators. This does not mean that harmful, deviant, or criminal acts have not been carried out. Thus, a large proportion of criminal activity is erroneously excluded from the data set. In addition, by accepting state definitions of crime and deviance, biological positivists ignore the fact that ruling groups define what is considered criminal and thus the laws are less likely to focus on or include the harmful activities regularly undertaken by elites. In addition, many of the people in prison would have been wrongly convicted, therefore, not people who had committed crimes at all. Lombroso's research, if sound, should have been able to identify the wrongly accused among the atavists but it could not. By ignoring these facts, biological positivists are not explaining crime and deviance. They are merely describing who is more likely to be arrested in a class-based and unequal social system.

The studies of many of the positivists do not live up to their own claims to scientific soundness. They are largely methodologically deficient and provide unsubstantiated results. For example, Lombroso and Sheldon drew their samples from people who were already criminalized. They did not use appropriate random sampling techniques drawing subjects from the general population. Their research thus lacked any predictive capacities. The positivists used a circular reasoning that simply said that people in prison were considered criminals. But no study was needed to tell a researcher that people already in prison might be "criminals" or at least have been criminalized. Studies that claimed to be scientific failed to follow scientific methods.

Third, the positivist theories provide overly deterministic models of human behavior. All of criminal behavior is reduced to one limited cause. Social factors are excluded even as conditioning variables that might contribute to certain behaviors. By looking at individual biology or psychology, the positivists avoid addressing larger questions such as the role that class plays in nutrition or health. It also overlooks the role that profiling plays in surveillance and detection of people who might be charged with crimes. Partly related to their improper methods they are not able to control for, or account for, other variables, such as the environment that might have given rise either to specific physical characteristics or to criminal activity itself. Poverty, or wealth, might affect one's body type as well as one's need to engage in crime or ability to get away with it.

Conclusion

One should be cautious of all claims to "scientific objectivity" in analyses of social and political issues. All social scientists, and their research, is driven by, supported by, and reinforced by specific interests that are social in nature. Research is influenced by the positionality of the researcher within social structures of class, power, and inequality. Whether specific ideas are disseminated widely and taken up publicly is largely an outcome of these same social structures.

Positivist theories have been taken up, and gained dominance, largely because they tell stories that social power holders want to hear. They reinforce the biases and prejudices of elites and explain social issues in terms that economic and political elites find to be agreeable. These are stories of crime and deviance being the result almost exclusively of the behaviors of non-elites. Even more, the biological makeup of working class deviants is said to be distinct from elites whose activities are not associated with crime and deviance. The physical characteristics of working class people are associated with criminal activity. Yet positivist researchers can draw no correspondence with the physical attributes of economic elites (perhaps soft hands, lack of calluses, manicured fingernails) because positivist theories did not consider the harmful activities of elites (pollution, workplace injuries, insider trading, embezzlement, and so on) to be crimes. Their assumptions that crime is street crime and that street crimes are committed by non-elites predetermines their analysis and its conclusions.

CHAPTER 5

Social Structure Theories

S ocial structure theories bring a sociological, rather than biological or psychological, approach to studies of crime and deviance. Instead of focusing solely or primarily on individuals, social structural theories seek to explain how individuals are situated within and experience larger scale social institutions such as schools, government, the labour market, cultural industries and the criminal justice system. There have emerged mainstream or consensus theories of social structure as well as critical or conflict theories of structure. For mainstream or consensus theories, social structures serve to regulate and socialize individuals to conform to dominant social norms, rewarding some behaviors while penalizing others. Within critical social structure theories; social, economic, and political power are understood as structures that form barriers impeding, constraining, or shaping what is possible for people in specific societal contexts, largely according to class, ethnicity, gender, or sexuality.

Early Sociological Theory: The Work of Ferdinand Tönnies

Sociology as an organized approach to understanding human society emerged in the turmoil and strife of the late nineteenth and early twentieth centuries, as was the case with other academic disciplines of the so-called "social sciences" such as psychology and criminology. This period was marked by rapid industrial development in the Industrial Revolution, mass production, and social conflict based around struggles between social classes (proletariat and bourgeoisie), and new forms of political mobilization in mass movements of labour. In addition, movements demanding increased access to justice and respect for previously oppressed groups, especially women and racialized communities, gathered strength and challenged social elites. This was also a period of substantial cultural change marked most notably by the large scale movement of populations from rural to urban areas, urbanization, and the migration of people internationally. These migrations brought about major cultural transformations, bringing large numbers of people from diverse backgrounds into close proximity in expanding urban and suburban areas. Other important transformations included the introduction and spread of new, mass technologies, from the telegraph to the radio to television, which allowed for the rapid transmission of information across great distances and which shifted communication from local to national and even global levels. Taken together, these many economic, political, and social transformations represent conditions of what social theorists came to call modernity — urban, technologically advanced and industry based, multicultural, mass societies. Early sociologists sought to understand the structures and processes that drove these modernist societies, how they were developing and changing, and what benefits and threats they might pose to human well being, individually and socially.

Among the first to apply sociological analysis to understand these broad social transformations was the German sociologist Ferdinand Tönnies (1855-1936). To explain social activities within modern, industrial societies, Tönnies draws a distinction between two primary social orders — *gemeinschaft* and *gesellschaft* — and compares and contrasts the characteristics that distinguish one form of social organization from the other. These social arrangements are marked by different degrees of solidarity, cooperation, and conflict. One is more prone to conflict and crime than the other. Roughly speaking, *gemeinschaft* is associated with community while *gesellschaft* is associated with society.

In Tönnies' conceptualization, *gemeinschaft* is the form of social order that characterizes rural, agrarian communities, such as peasant villages under feudalism. Such communities are marked by a low division of labour, sharing of resources and mutual aid, closeness and familiarity of group members, and strong feelings of solidarity and support within the group. Indeed, in rural communities people know their neighbours, often over generations, and they have to work together and share labour and resources or the community will not survive. If you are sick, you need to rely on your neighbours to do the planting or harvest the crops.

Chapter 5: Social Structure Theories

The other form of social organization outlined by Tönnies is termed *gesell-schaft* and is characteristic of social life in industrial capitalist systems. Social relations within *gesellschaft* contexts are characterized by individualism; impersonal interactions based on money, and instrumental or opportunistic treatment of others. In *gesellschaft* contexts, people view their interlocutors as simply "ahead" rather than out of care or sentiments of solidarity or mutual aid as is common within *gemeinschaft* contexts. People use other people as instruments for their own benefit. Within *gesellschaft* societies, as under capitalism, money is the key means of interaction with other people. Over time, pursuit of money comes to dominate other concerns, and becomes more important than the proper treatment of people. Exploitation becomes the basis for social life. Think about the number of anonymous, impersonal, instrumental interactions and relationships you have every day, in which you deal with people solely or primarily on the basis of monetary exchange in which you are trying to get something. Interactions with shopkeepers, service workers, cashiers, or receptionists would provide ample examples.

In *gemeinschaft* arrangements, people are motivated by an "essential will" and see themselves as making contributions to the greater good or the broader community. *Gesellschaft* societies encourage an "arbitrary will" in which people see the broader social group as a means to satisfy their own personal wants. *Gesellschaft* societies, based on competition, instrumentalism, and monetary gain, in which people have less familiarity with their neighbours and less generational continuity (where families grow up together over generations) are more prone to crime, conflict, and violence. The informal means of social stability that hold communities together in *gemeinschaft* contexts — such as familiarity, family ties, mutual aid, and dependence on neighbours for subsistence, shared morals and norms — are largely absent within *gesellschaft* contexts. Instead, *gesellschaft* societies rely on formal institutions, laws, courts, police, and prisons, that are separate and distant from the people that they regulate and which tend to deal with problems reactively, or after the fact, rather than proactively or on a preventative basis.

Critical theories, which will be explored later, have taken up Tönnies' analysis to argue that capitalist societies, rather than being subjected to crime, actually create crime and the conditions for crime. Thus, the higher crime rates noted in advanced capitalist societies like the U.S.

Emile Durkheim and Functionalism:
Solidarity and *Anomie*

Mainstream or consensus-based social structure theories trace their roots to the work of the French sociologist Emile Durkheim (1858-1917). For Durkheim, crime is a social rather than psychological social phenomenon and the product of a specific kind of social order. As for other early sociologists, Durkheim is concerned about the emergence of industrial capitalist societies and the transformation involved in the shift from rural, agrarian communities to urban, industrial societies. He attempts to understand the impacts on social relations and institutions of a shift from one type of social order to another. A key concept for Durkheim in understanding the broader arrangement of social life is the division of labour. Modern societies are characterized by important changes in the division of labour, unique in human history, and this has significant ramifications for social institutions as well as cultural and moral practices. Indeed the connectedness between social structures and the norms, values, and beliefs in a given society, and the need to understand these connections (rather than privileging one over the other), is a central aspect of Durkheim's work. It would establish important lessons for sociological analyses to follow.

In his influential book *The Division of Labour in Society* (1893), Durkheim argues that the key aspect of societies is the division of labour or the way in which specific work, tasks, or roles are structured and distributed. For Durkheim, the division of labour will shape the relationships and interactions within society and thus makes up a central part of any social analysis. Durkheim distinguishes between mechanical solidarity and organic solidarity based on different degrees of the division of labour exhibited by social groupings. These correspond in various ways with Tönnies' concepts of *gemeinschaft* and *gesellschaft*.

Mechanical solidarity characterizes social relationships in non-industrial, rural, agrarian communities. It is typical of social groupings with a low division of labour. People, as in agricultural communities such as peasant villages, have similar skills and engage in similar tasks, labour, or roles. They also tend to share norms, values, and beliefs which are often passed on from generation to generation. It is marked by homogeneity or sameness. There is much community familiarity, people know their neighbours, and the community pulls together to meet important needs, such as getting the crops in. Community relations are based on cooperation and mutual aid which is enhanced because the lower division of labour means people can step in to perform a task for someone who is unable. The term mechanical is used because people respond mechanically to requirements imposed by nature such as food or shelter.

Organic solidarity, on the other hand, describes the sorts of social relationships that mark mass industrial capitalist societies. The division of labour within capitalist societies is extremely diverse and differentiated by tasks, labour, or roles. There is a great deal of specialization in tasks. Any city might have thousands of different and distinct job roles, from actor to baker to garbage collector to doctor to professor to secretary to zoologist. Any given factory might have a thousand different job descriptions as the task, say assembling an automobile, is divided into minute, distinct tasks, from brake assembly to electrical inspection. Not only is a high division of labour associated with great variation in tasks, it is also associated with important differences in norms, values, beliefs, and worldviews.

Societies with a high — diverse and complex — division of labour are more likely to exhibit higher rates of crime, conflict, and violence as people within society have fewer shared experiences, connections, and interests. An unhealthy division of labour is one in which people are not rewarded for their skills with appropriate roles, or where they are not able to access roles suited to their aptitude due to prejudice, bias, or class inequalities that restrict people's opportunities or life chances. Racism, patriarchy, economic stratification can all have an effect. Notably, in societies with a high division of labour, there are great disparities in status and wealth within the society. Accountants have higher status than garbage collectors, despite the fact that the latter may do more important and essential work. In addition, there are different levels of remuneration associated with these different roles. This can fuel resentment and conflict. Furthermore within societies with a high division of labour, there can emerge competition between members of different sectors of society. One may feel greater loyalty or commitment to their sector or profession than to society as a whole or to people in other sectors or jobs. These divisions can spur conflict and opposition within society leading to a range of social problems. During the financial crisis of 2008, representatives of the auto industry conflicted with resource sectors, such as logging companies in British Columbia, as each argued that they, not the other, deserved government bailouts. In situations like this different sectors can work to pursue their own interests rather than the interests of society as a whole, thereby creating strife and further crisis.

The degree or level of the division of labour impacts the belief and value systems of the society. These impacts can affect the health of society, becoming manifest in levels of conflict or crime. Specifically, a society without shared norms and values will function poorly. For Durkheim, all societies, no matter how large or small, are regulated by a *conscience collective*, shared norms, beliefs, rituals, and customs, that holds their diverse members together, providing a shared worldview or value system that structures acceptable and unacceptable social behaviors. This shapes and regulates social interactions. The notion of *conscience collective* suggests that social groupings express a collective or shared consciousness that is greater than the consciousness of an individual, or sum of individual consciousness, and shapes behavior within society. For Durkheim, small-scale societies, such as horticultural or agricultural societies, with a low level of social differentiation and a minimal division of labour, where the majority of society share similar life experiences, exhibit the strongest and most durable *conscience collective* and thus the least occurrences of crime and deviance. Within industrial capitalist societies, which are characterized by a broad and diverse division of labour, the *conscience collective* is more difficult to sustain given the great social and cultural differences that exist and disparities in wealth and social opportunity. Again, similar to Tönnies' discussion, mechanical solidarity relies on cultural conformity and face-to-face regulation of behavior, while organic solidarity relies on abstract laws and formal, authoritarian, institutions like police, courts, and prisons to regulate social life. A breakdown of shared values, increased by a growing division of labour, leads to what Durkheim calls *anomie*, or a condition of normlessness. *Anomie* results in increased crime, deviance, and suicide rates.

Durkheim provides a memorable and influential example of how his analytical approach can be deployed to aid understanding of social problems in perhaps his most famous work, *Suicide* (1897). During the period in which Durkheim wrote, the period of turmoil marking the late nineteenth and early twentieth centuries, suicide was a problem of growing concern. Durkheim used a sociological approach to understand what was typically presented as an individual problem, an outcome of personal psychological pathology. If suicide was simply an individual psychological problem, it should be relatively evenly distributed throughout the population, not varying much by residence or religion. Yet, using statistical data from several European countries, Durkheim revealed that suicide was not evenly distributed among the population and, in fact, people in specific life situations were committing suicide more frequently than others.

Chapter 5: Social Structure Theories

He identified three characteristics that were associated with suicide rates. First, city dwellers, particularly residents of larger cities, were more likely to commit suicide than were people in smaller towns or villages. Second, people who lived alone were more likely to commit suicide than people who had strong family ties and lived in larger domestic groups. Third, people who practiced Catholic religion, with an emphasis on communal relations, committed suicide less frequently than practitioners of Protestant religions, with an emphasis on the individual. What would explain these particular variations? For Durkheim, explanations based on individual psychology or a pathology of character would not suffice. In his view all of these factors were expressions of the degree of social connection. People who were part of closer communities, or had stronger family ties, or lived in settings that had more familiarity with neighbours, rather than anonymous settings as in urban areas, were less likely to commit suicide. Social integration can sustain people better than social isolation, and understanding an issue such as suicide requires an analysis of social factors that might otherwise be overlooked in approaches that focus only on the individual (rationality or biology).

Notably, Durkheim shifts the emphasis away from the individual and toward social structures and processes. The breakdown of norms is a result of social rather than individual factors. Even more, dominant, accepted norms, values, and beliefs might actually contribute to the emergence of crime and deviance. Where dominant values encourage or legitimize an unequal or unhealthy division of labour, rather than supporting necessary changes, they can help create conditions either for crime and deviance or rebellion and resistance. Again, social rather than individual factors are key. Crime is a social phenomenon and the result of specific types of social order. Society is more than the sum of its individual parts.

Durkheim's approach is often referred to as functionalist. He seeks explanations for issues like conflict, crime, and deviance in the specific institutions and structures of particular societies rather than the personal characteristics of individual people. To understand crime and deviance, it is necessary to look at society as a whole, as an interlocking system, and the relationships that exist between independent parts of the social system. Crime and deviance, like other social behaviors, are functional within the society in which they occur — they serve a purpose, whether to highlight deeper problems or to point to possible solutions or necessary reorganizations of social life.

Strain Theories

Durkheim's work has informed a range of social structure theories, including the influential work of Robert K. Merton and Albert Cohen. During the 1950s and 1960s, structural theories represented the dominant sociological perspective on crime and deviance. First among these was Merton's "strain theory." According to Merton, individuals in capitalist societies like the U.S. share essentially the same cultural goals, namely wealth, status, and financial success. This is the so-called American Dream. These goals are encouraged and reinforced by the major social institutions, such as schools, government, media, and corporations. As well there are culturally preferred and encouraged means to achieve these goals, particularly, education, hard work, thrift and personal sacrifice. These become culturally valued attributes or practices, expressed in notions such as the so-called "work ethic." Unfortunately, people have differential means available for achieving these culturally supported goals. Some have blocked opportunities, particularly because of class location or socio-economic status, but also because of race, ethnicity or gender discrimination, and are unable to achieve their goals through legitimate means. Society offers members of different social groups very different institutional means, such as unequal opportunities for education regardless of ability, fulfilling work, or financial aid. Strain develops from this means-end discrepancy between culturally encouraged goals and structurally available means for achieving them, and can result in deviance. A gap between effort and reward makes it impossible for some people to set realistic, achievable goals or to plan legitimate ways of achieving their goals. This strain creates conditions of *anomie,* according to Merton. Here he means frustration or stress rather than the breakdown of norms that Durkheim meant by the term.

According to Merton, individuals respond to this strain in one of five ways. First is conformism in which people accept the socially encouraged means and ends. They stay in school and sacrifice to become economically successful. The second option is innovation, in which people accept the goals of wealth and status but reject the means. An example would be drug dealers or corporate criminals who pursue illegal means or cheat to achieve financial success. The third option involves ritualism in which people become attached to the means but lose sight of the goals. A "professional student" or middle management bureaucrat might be examples of ritualism. Fourth is retreatism, in which people reject both the means and goals. A dropout or someone who pursues subcultural activities might be an example of retreatism. Finally, there are rebels, those who reject the socially defined goals and means but seek to replace them with alternatives. Revolutionaries, anarchists, and counter-cultural activists would exemplify rebellion. According to Merton, those of lower socioeconomic status are most likely to experience greater strain and therefore engage in deviant acts such as retreatism or innovation.

This was for many years the dominant theory of crime and deviance. It has not held up to closer scrutiny and empirical testing. Many dropouts and rebels are middle class youth who have wonderful access to accepted means and are well socialized to accept societal goals. The theory also fails to explain why people choose one strategy over another. It also has little to say about elite deviance or corporate crime, which it largely overlooks.

Many theorists have developed structural theories building upon Merton's work. Albert Cohen focused specifically on working class youth. He presented the notion of status frustration to explain higher rates of delinquency among youth from less wealthy backgrounds. In his view, frustration results from the fact that poorer youth lack sufficient access to legitimate means to achieve their goals and recognize this. This recognition is expressed in social frustration, and a sense that they will be punished no matter how they behave, and is acted upon through acts of deviance.

Richard Cloward and Lloyd Ohlin suggest that marginalized youth seek alternatives or innovations to seek their goals. Youth face "differential opportunity structures" that limit their life options and possibilities for personal development. As a result, these youth form and join subcultures to help themselves achieve their goals or develop alternatives. Their work focuses on the emergence of deviant subcultures among youth.

Over the last few decades a variety of authors have focused on economic structures and the emergence of deviance. Robert Agnew's "general strain theory" explains deviance as a coping mechanism to help adolescents deal with the negative emotional states related to their experiences of socioeconomic problems. Proponents of "institutional strain theory" note that throughout the neo-liberal era, roughly from the 1980s to the present, economic issues have come to dominate non-economic spheres, weakening the informal control mechanisms exerted by the family, school, church, and communities. Politics becomes about the economy, trade and investment rather than social policy, civil rights or democratic practice. School, for example, is now dominated by considerations of the job market and employability, rather than concerns for critical thought or citizenship. Programs that are viewed as contributing to personal enrichment rather than employability such as music, drama, art, classical studies, or philosophy face cuts or cancellation in favour of trades and technology or business training. For institutional strain theory, the heightened emphasis on success in economic terms increases social strain or anomie. The emphasis on the most expedient path to economic success means that crime may be viewed as the most efficient means to financial gain. The celebrity status achieved by corporate criminals, such as Michael Milken during the Reagan era, provides but one example for institutional strain theorists.

Positive Aspects of Deviance

For many structuralist theorists, including Durkheim and Albert Cohen, deviance and crime can actually be positive for society. In his influential book *The Rules of Sociological Method* (1895), Durkheim suggests that crime is an inevitable occurrence in any society. In fact, Durkheim argues that a certain amount of crime is actually required by every society.

Deviance will occur within any society because not all of the members of society are equally committed to the *conscience collective*. Some will question or reject the overarching norms, values, or beliefs of society and there will be public expressions of disagreement or dissent. Even more such disagreement and dissent is healthy, and productive, for society. In Durkheim's view, those societies that exhibit particularly low levels of deviance may, in fact, be less healthy that those societies in which somewhat greater degrees or types of deviance are on display. While most accounts in the public discourses of contemporary liberal democracies depict deviant as a sign of unhealthy societies, Durkheim suggests the opposite.

Real problems with deviance only emerge in those cases in which the degree of crime becomes overwhelming or extreme, such that it leads to ongoing conflict and threatens the stability and development of society. Such might be the case in societies dominated by unsanctioned militias, thugs, or "men with guns."

It is only through engagement with deviance, and the consideration of new or alternative ideas and practices, that society progresses or develops. Otherwise

Chapter 5: Social Structure Theories

society would be left to stagnate or even regress in the absence of alternatives and innovations. Too tight control over behavior and ideas will suffocate creativity and stamp out novel approaches to addressing social needs. Functionalist sociologists argue that some of the greatest social improvements experienced in human communities have resulted from acts that violate laws. Among these are acts of civil disobedience in pursuit of civil rights, anti-war movements, ecology movements, and women's rights, to mention only a few. These include acts of willful or intentional deviance. The history of social justice is a history of challenging and rejecting unjust laws and rules that sustain oppression and exploitation. Often, rules are not appropriate and laws are not what they should be.

The history of science — experimentation, invention, revision — would never have progressed without large degrees of deviance, and even crime. Science, almost by definition, could not advance without the exploration and testing of unaccepted ideas and practices. Science also challenges accepted authorities and calls for new ways of producing and sharing knowledge. Indeed, much scientific activity has been subjected to surveillance, restriction, and silencing by state and religious authorities who feared and opposed the development of new idea systems that challenged the taken-for-granted order of things. Galileo Galilei, the Italian physicist, astronomer, mathematician, and philosopher, who is considered by many to be the central figure in the founding of modern physics, was tried by the Roman Inquisition which found him suspect of heresy. His transgression? Galileo supported the idea, and provided evidence, that the Earth orbited the Sun (heliocentrism) rather than the religious view that the Sun orbited the Earth (geocentrism). For this, Galileo was sentenced to house arrest for the rest of his life (dying after nine years), his book arguing the case for heliocentrism was banned, and it was forbidden to publish any of his books, including future ones. Yet where would society and science be if the belief that the Earth stood still in space while the Sun moved around it still held sway? Even less tasteful activities have advanced knowledge and benefited human life. Much of the early modern study of biology and anatomy developed through grave robbery and the use of stolen cadavers, as troubling as that may seem. This is not to advocate grave robbery but simply to question absolutist approaches to issues of crime and deviance.

For Durkheim, deviance can provide a catalyst of spur for positive social change and growth in society. One can see the impact of social change if one considers that activities that were once viewed as deviant or unacceptable, such as single parenthood or same-sex relationships, are now viewed as positive or acceptable. Not only does deviance give rise to social change and progress, it results from it. People within vibrant and dynamic societies may experience confusion or uncertainty over new or changing norms, values, and beliefs and may, as a result, transgress notions of the acceptable and unacceptable in emerging ideas or practices.

Functionalist sociologists, including Durkheim and those influenced by Durkheim, argue that deviance can provide an incredibly important, but unappreciated, service to society. They identify a variety of possible social benefits associated with deviance. Six of these positive contributions of deviance or crime are examined next.

First, deviance can serve to cut through red tape. An organization may, at times, require the bending or breaking of its own rules in order to achieve its stated goals. Unquestioning conformity to rules may, in practice, defeat an organization's capacity to function properly or efficiently. Think about the movement of resources in times of emergency, such as during Hurricane Katrina or the British Petroleum spill in the Gulf of Mexico recently. If all of the rules were followed to the letter, important resources and supplies would not reach people who needed them. In times of crisis, bending and breaking the rules become necessities for survival. Rigid adherence to the rules could cost lives.

Second, deviance or crime, at least lower level forms, can act as a safety valve for the release of ongoing tensions that characterize social life on an everyday basis. Particularly in diverse, large scale societies that are unequally structured and stratified along lines of class, patriarchy, and racism, tensions and resentments can build up within different sectors of people. Left unchecked, these tensions and pressures could explode in extreme violence and conflict. Moments of deviance, crime or "acting out" can serve to allow people to "blow off steam" in a way that is not overly harmful or dangerous. Riots can offer an example of this where they destroy some property but do not challenge broader property relations or relations of ruling. Many cultures, in fact, include regular moments of "patterned norm evasion" or "moral holidays" that permit at least occasional and/or ritual rule breaking. In these moments the regular rules do not apply. Examples of popular and well known moral holidays include Mardi Gras, holiday partying, casinos, 420, or Halloween. Indeed countries like Canada and the U.S. have entire locations that are sites of

Chapter 5: Social Structure Theories

ongoing moral holiday, including Las Vegas, New Orleans, and Niagara Falls. Of course, from a critical or radical perspective, deviance is even more beneficial where it actually does challenge and change property and power relations.

Third, acts of deviance and criminality can serve to clarify social rules, particularly around issues for which perspectives are changing or there is much debate or controversy. In such cases of controversy or disagreement, deviance can resolve ambiguities about the status or meaning of a rule. Deviances can force a social grouping either to abandon a rule in question or reaffirm it if it is still valued. The moments of clarification serve to let other members of the group find out what people might think should or should not be done about the rule. One example, from recent Canadian history, involves abortion and a woman's right to choose whether to proceed with a pregnancy or not. During the 1960s, as a result of social movements mobilizing and arguing for women's rights and control by women over their own bodies, as well as the limiting of state involvement in matters of personal choice, began to impact perceptions of abortion. Attitudes about abortion were changing, becoming more accepting, yet abortion was still criminalized. In this context, women openly advocated for the laws to change. To force the issue and to test society's values on the issue, Dr. Henry Morgentaler openly performed abortions challenging the state to intervene if the opposition to abortion was still a social value. Following his arrests and trials, it became apparent that values around abortion had changed and thus the laws were changed. The act of deviance or crime forces society to choose. If the issue is no longer a public concern, change the laws and stop criminalizing the activity. Similar processes have occurred around same-sex marriage, marijuana use, sex work, and assisted suicide.

In addition, when someone is learning the rules associated with a new social role, there will be moments of experimentation with behavior that tests or transgresses the borderline. This can offer suggestions around how the role might be effectively changed, revised, or improved. People engaging in such activities can encourage a group to make decisions about unclear rules or roles or to introduce innovations.

Fourth, deviance can serve to enhance group solidarity in societies in which people often remain anonymous, detached, or distant with regard to others, including even neighbours. In mass societies, societies of organic solidarity or gesellschaft, people may not interact closely with people in their cities or regions and may have little opportunity to come together to discuss and debate issues or mobilize collective and participatory solutions to address concerns in their communities. Crime can provide a catalyst to bring people together and can lead to expressions of solidarity and mutual aid. This can happen in two ways. First people might organize together to improve a situation in their community that has given rise to crime. This might involve assisting someone who has committed a crime out of personal distress or it might mean building community infrastructures that might prevent similar crimes from happening in the future. In the second case, it might involve coming together to protect someone who has been charged with a criminal or deviant act and may face unjust punishment. In either case, people join together to deal with a perceived threat or to protect someone who has been identified as a threat. Without the occurrence of crime or deviance, people might stay within their own bubbles and not interact, or only interact minimally, with the people around them.

Fifth, deviance or crime can serve as a reference point for society, reminding people about norms, values, and beliefs about issues that may not be discussed on a regular basis. In response to criminality or deviance, people may be reminded what roles are appropriate or inappropriate in society (or what roles might now be viewed differently than they were previously when the rule or law was implemented). In mass societies where people do not have much opportunity to meet or know most of the people they live near, as in major urban centres, or where there is little opportunity to participate in policy making, crime and deviance, and the response to them, may provide the only clear sense of how people generally feel about or perceive an issue. Deviance provides the reference point for evaluating appropriate behaviors and activities. Crime and deviance, rather than dividing a community may actually contribute to a broader or stronger sense of moral community or connectedness.

Sixth, deviance or crime can serve as a warning signal about greater, more serious, underlying tensions and problems that may be about to surface in dangerous or harmful ways. Deviance can be a signal that something is wrong with the rules, i.e. they may be unjust, or that the organization of society has a fundamental problem that must be resolved before social life more broadly is threatened. Riots, for example, often express the fact that social injustice or inequality has reached a breaking point and will no longer be tolerated. If the underlying problem is not addressed, greater turmoil, conflict, or violence may ensue. Illegal protests or civil disobedience show that large numbers of society will no longer sit by quietly and accept injustice, as was true in the case

Chapter 5: Social Structure Theories

of the civil rights movements in the U.S. during the 1960s. In these cases, as in others, the so-called deviant or criminal, by putting themselves on the line and facing state violence, arrest, and/or detention is often acting to benefit much larger numbers of people who support the act but are unable or afraid to act and thus suffer in silence.

Societies with extremely low levels of crime are likely societies that are stagnant and lacking in innovation. They are typically societies in which dissent is not tolerated and social injustice and shared prejudices are not contested. Such societies lack vitality and tend to be characterized by suppression and authoritarianism. For example, if one wants to look at recent instances of societies with extremely low levels of deviance and crime (excluding state executed crimes) and little tolerance for dissent or disagreement, one might refer to Nazi Germany and Stalinist Russia. Notably, in both cases, the political states engaged in high levels of horrific crimes, indeed crimes against humanity. In Nazi Germany, the government carried out the mass murder or genocide of entire populations, including the Jewish and Roma communities, in the course of the Holocaust. As well the arrests, detention, and torture of political opponents were regular state activities. In Stalinist Russia, again, mass executions, arrests, detention, and torture were regularly carried out by state organizations. Charges of genocide, as in the mass starvation of Ukrainians, have also been leveled against the Stalinist regime. Notably, these societies also tolerated very little political dissent, artistic variety, or cultural difference. Intellectuals and artists were stifled, silenced, and executed on the whims of state authorities. The civilian crime rates in these two very different and distinct societies were extremely low compared to those of their neighbours, yet neither was the type of society that anyone reading this book would view as healthy, desirable, or enviable. Would you want to live there?

So we always need to be cautious about calls from state representatives to stamp out deviance and crime. We should think through what that might mean in actual practice, particularly if the state gets to decide what is criminal or deviant, who should be held accountable, and how.

Critical Structure Theories

For more critical or radical proponents of structural theories, there is a problem with the emphasis that is often placed on street crimes or the crimes of the working class within mainstream structural theories. First, the most harmful crimes, socially and environmentally, are crimes of elites, such as toxic dumping, unsafe products, unhealthy working conditions, pollution and food contamination, and these should be given more attention than the small-scale crimes that take up most of criminal justice system resources. Second, the use of criminal justice statistics, such as police and court records, within some of the structural theories identified above, misrepresents actual criminal activity. The use of police records in social ecology theories to calculate neighbourhood crime rates, reflects police surveillance of those neighbourhoods rather than actual rates of criminal activity. Finally, while structural theories do a good job of documenting social inequalities, critical theorists argue that the point is to confront and end inequality.

For critical structural theorists, including structural Marxism and anarchism, the main structures in society that must be understood in relation to crime and deviance, are the state and capital. These are the institutions that fundamentally control social resources and have the power to define specific acts as crimes or certain individuals as criminals, often on the basis of class or other factors. The capitalist state and its institutions exist to preserve the interests of the dominant economic class, the capitalist class of those who own and control the means of production. The main concern of this dominant class is the preservation of an economic and social order that maintains their privilege and allows them to continue the accumulation of wealth. Behaviors that threaten the existing socioeconomic regime are most likely to be targeted, ideologically as well as practically, for punishment. Thus, most resources of the criminal justice system are directed toward, often minor, property crimes such as petty thefts and shoplifting. Similarly, moral panics are most often directed toward the activities of the working class and poor, particularly working class youth, e.g. raves, squeegeeing, hip hop, punk. Crimes of elites, such as corporate crime, ecological crimes, or government misconduct receive far less attention from the criminal justice system and result in fewer, and less severe, punishments. The main focus of the criminal justice system, according to critical structural theorists, is to prohibit behaviors that threaten the unequal distribution of property under capitalism or the state's monopoly on the use of force. Thus, the criminalization of union organizing, strikes, protests, and rebellion. The inherent conflicts that exist within a system of broad socioeconomic inequality are controlled through the structures of government and the criminal justice system in a way that inhibits disadvantaged classes and sustains dominant classes' capacities to rule. For structural Marxists, the state must be taken over and controlled by the working class to serve their needs. For anarchists the state, as an inherently authoritarian and hierarchical institution, is always a force of domination and cannot be used to achieve equality. Instead the state must be replaced by community-based direct democracy and participatory decision-making.

CHAPTER 6

Sociology in the Streets: Social Ecology and Social Disorganization

One of the criticisms of structural theories, such as those examined in the previous chapter, is that they operate at too high a level of abstraction. That is to say that they often speak in too general terms about broad, large-scale structures that are distant from the specificity of people's everyday lives. Someone might live in a *gesellschaft* society, a society that exhibits the characteristics described by Tönnies, in general but specific experiences, environments, and relationships with various *gesellschaft* societies will vary. Not all are the same in detail or are organized in the same way. There are important distinctions between life in twenty-first century Canada and life in twentieth century England, for example. Even more, not all locations in a given *gesellschaft* society, for example, are the same in structure or behaviors. No one lives in Canada the national entity. People live in, and experience, different regions, towns, cities, environments within the larger context and those specific locations are probably more meaningful at various points in people's lives than the larger, more abstract, national context.

Theorists have sought more local and rooted levels of analysis that draw out and examine the specific contexts in which people operate on a day-to-day basis. One of the key locations for human activity within modern urban societies is the neighbourhood. In cities like Vancouver, for example, there is great neighbourhood variation across the city. Life in Kitsilano, a gentrified upscale neighbourhood in the city's west end, is not the same as life in the Downtown Eastside, the poorest neighbourhood in Canada, or Commercial Drive, an area that has long been home to close-knit alternative and activist communities.

Things are very different in suburban areas of Metro Vancouver like Surrey, which in turn differs from Richmond, for example.

Beginning roughly in the 1910s, a variety of sociologists sought to locate human behavior, and analyze it, in the specific day-to-day context of the neighbourhood. This offered a mid-level or meso level of analysis, adding important details to the macro level works of the structural theorists.

Many theorists, still paying close attention to social structures, have preferred to examine links between crime and levels of disorganization within specific neighbourhoods or communities rather than more abstract cultural values or institutions. Social ecology theories, influenced by the Chicago School of Sociology and the work of Robert E. Park (1864-1944), suggest that in crime-ridden neighbourhoods local institutions such as schools and social service agencies have broken down and no longer perform their expected or stated functions. Residents experience conflict and despair, and antisocial behavior results. High rates of school dropout and high youth unemployment are typical characteristics of breakdown leading to deviance and crime.

According to "cultural transmission theory," poor neighbourhoods are marked by high population turnover rates and this disrupts informal social controls. Such areas are said to give rise to youth crime. Crime will be a constant feature in such areas regardless of the personal character of the residents because of existing structural conditions. In addition, according to "cultural transmission theory," gang activity and youth deviance are normal and expected responses to adverse conditions in which legitimized alternatives are otherwise not available for youth who perceive themselves trapped without options. For these theories, crime is a strategy to deal with destructive social conditions.

The Second City: Chicago

One of the first schools of sociology in North America developed at the University of Chicago. Using a range of empirical methods (those based on observation and/or experimentation) to study society, the Chicago School would influence research far beyond the academic discipline of sociology — contributing to theory and research in areas of social psychology and urban studies. A main premise of the Chicago School is that crime and deviance are rooted in the unique characteristics of particular neighbourhoods. Crime and deviance are shaped by the everyday structures and relations within areas of the city that most express characteristics of disorganization, population turn-over, resource deficits, and lack of shared values. To test their theories, they approached the city of Chicago, their own city, as a laboratory of human behavior and interaction.

One of the key themes of this book is that theories are rooted in particular contexts and reflect the struggles, conflicts, and relations of power that mark those contexts. This is true of social ecology theories as for others discussed already. In the case of early social ecology theories, the specific context is not so much regional or national as it is the unique developmental history of a specific urban centre. Chicago in the late 1800s and early 1900s experienced what may have been the most rapid growth of any city in U.S. history to the present (Grossman, Keating, and Reiff 2005). Economic expansion fueled a population boom in Chicago. Within a very short period of time at the dawn of the twentieth century, Chicago's population increased from around 300,000 to almost 1.7 million (Grossman, Keating, and Reiff 2005). It saw rapid industrialization and the enormous influx of people from different regions of not only the U.S., but the world.

In the urban environment of Chicago, people from different cultural, religious, and ethnic groups were brought together in close proximity, in apartments, on streets, in workplaces, often without even a shared language. Different, even opposing, norms, values, and beliefs came together in close contact and were differently received. New arrivals gravitated to the lower rent housing of neighbourhoods near the downtown city centre. These were areas of deteriorating housing and insufficient social resources. Thus, large and growing numbers of poor people, many from European countries, were concentrated in unsuitable housing in older neighbourhoods. Social dissatisfaction among residents was expressed in social reform movements. The needs of the poor were met by indifference or, as frequently, hostility from economic and political elites.

The hostility of elites, and their contempt for the poor, was exacerbated by Social Darwinist sentiments that equated European migrants with cultural and ethnic inferiority. European migrants were held to be morally degenerate and given to criminality. Even more, Europeans were associated with political radicalism and blamed for labour unrest, rather than the obvious causes of awful working conditions and miniscule wages.

This was certainly a period, encompassing the Industrial Revolution, of great class conflict as workers seeking better working and living conditions opposed powerful industrialists backed by governments and institutions of the criminal justice system that acted to protect the claims of elites to property and profit. Class struggle, rather than hidden away in workplaces, was often open, and often violent. Working people recognized that they were being exploited by business owners and organized to improve their lives and escape the exploitative conditions of their labour, not only through improved working conditions but through calls for workers' control of the industries in which they worked.

Chicago was the site of some of the most vicious crackdowns by state forces, police and military, against labour organizing and unions. The first great struggles for the eight hour workday initiated in Chicago. These were often tumultuous and bloody struggles. In 1886, during a demonstration and rally for the eight-hour day, a dynamite bomb was thrown by an unknown person into a crowd assembled at Haymarket Square. What is known as the Haymarket Massacre left several people dead (mostly police killed by friendly fire), led to a violent wave of repression against labour and community organizers and union members. It resulted in the judicial frame up of eight people identified as anarchist labour organizers (George Engel, Samuel Fielden, Adolph Fischer, Louis Lingg, Oscar Neebe, Albert Parsons, Michael Schwab, and August Spies). Four were convicted and executed while a fifth committed suicide while in prison. All of this occurred despite that fact that the prosecution admitted that none of the defendants had actually thrown the bomb. Clearly the men were targeted because of their political perspectives and activities defending working people against exploitation by business owners. They were targeted because they posed a real or perceived threat to corporate property and profitability. The personal identities of the accused men are even more telling. Beyond being anarchist labour organizers, five of the men were German immigrants and another was of German descent. Another was an immigrant from England. Clearly, class intersected with ethnicity and national origin in the targeting of organizers for prosecution. At the time, elites expressed much concern publicly that immigrant radicals were "contaminating" the domestic workforce with supposedly foreign ideas like anarchism and socialism. Such claims have persisted throughout U.S. history, with echoes in Canada, as a means of discrediting labour and community organizers and presenting them and their ideas as outsiders or aliens.

Chapter 6: Sociology in the Streets: Social Ecology and Social Disorganization

The Haymarket Martyrs, as they have come to be known, were clearly innocent of the crimes of which they were accused, and for which five of them had
their lives taken. They were set up by the state, acting on behalf of business
owners, as scapegoats to serve as a warning to other labour and community
organizers, and the poor and oppressed more broadly, not to take up the struggle for working class justice and equality. The Haymarket Martyrs were killed
by the state largely because they held more radical views on social inequality
and injustice, including anarchist and Marxist perspectives. To say their perspectives were radical, if one looks at the origin of the term radical, simply
means that they went beyond surface explanations to get to the root of the
problem. In a sense, they employed a sociological perspective to understand
the condition of their lives and the lives of their neighbours and co-workers.

The frame up, show trials, and executions of the Haymarket Martyrs serve,
once again, as a reminder of the role of power in the selection, promotion,
dissemination, or silencing of ideas. It is a clear illustration of the part played
by powerful groups, economic and political elites, in the privileging of certain
ideas over others. It shows that those ideas that confront and challenge power
and authority within unequal societies face imposing, even lethal, obstacles
in gaining a broad public hearing. The history of ideas in capitalist societies is
filled with examples similar to the tragedy of the Haymarket Martyrs. Working
class and poor people who oppose exploitation and oppression are arrested,
defamed, and executed on a regular basis. Indeed, this is the unspoken story
of criminal (in)justice in class-based societies, including Canada and the U.S.

A Sociology of Disorganization: The Chicago School and Social Ecology

A key figure in the development of the sociology program at the University
of Chicago was Robert E. Park. Park played a crucial part in the development
of what is known as subcultural studies, the identification and analysis of
cultural groups and practices that differ from or oppose the dominant cultural groups and traditions in modern mass societies. Park was critical of detached and distant approaches to theorizing that produced abstract theory
that was disconnected from real lived experiences. He encouraged researchers
to go directly to the groups and people that they were interested in learning
about rather than studying from afar in the comfort of the university office or

armchair. His was an engaged and active approach to sociology. For Park, the social researcher who wants to know about crime and deviance should approach the issue with an open mind rather than prejudging people or dismissing them ahead of time for being "deviant" or "pathological." If one wants to understand deviant acts or behavior, one must understand why people engage in specific activities and what they derive from them, materially, psychologically, or emotionally. Go out and be part of the so-called deviant subculture. Immerse yourself in the subcultural milieu that you want to understand. See the world through the eyes of participants themselves.

The Chicago School, influenced by Park, engaged in a wide variety of ethnographic research. That is, they went "into the field" to observe directly and participate in the groups that they were interested in learning about. Some of this work would provide among the most insightful, fascinating, and exciting examples of sociological work ever produced. Memorable and influential accounts of alternative cultural practices produced through the encouragement of the Chicago School include Nels Andersen's *The Hobo* (1923) and Howard Becker's *Outsiders* (1963).

Among the innovations of the Chicago School was the study of the spatial organization of criminal activity. Using Chicago, a rapidly growing, diverse urban centre as an open laboratory for study, the Chicago School developed what is known as a social ecology of crime analysis. The Chicago School sought to explore and document the broad range of social groups and dynamics that animated city life. In doing so, they applied an ecological model of urban life to understand human behaviors on the basis of biological concepts such as selection, competition, and cooperation. In their view, increased social complexity, growing populations, and diversity of cultures gives rise to varying degrees of social disorganization.

One of the key claims of the social ecology approach is that crime is not randomly distributed across the urban environment. Criminal activity is shaped according to the particular geography and history of the specific neighbourhood in question. In Chicago, for example, they suggested that research would show that crime was not distributed evenly throughout the city but would vary between different neighbourhoods.

Chicago School researchers Robert E. Park and his colleague Ernest Burgess, argued that cities grew outward, like a tree or ripples on a pond, from the central business district or core. Moving outward from the central business district in concentric circles were other, later, zones of urban growth. These later developments include the transition zone, bordering the central business district, the working class zone, the residential zone, and, much later, the commuter zone or suburbs.

The "zone in transition" is the oldest residential zone in the city and grew up, often as working class housing, around the central business district. It becomes, over time, an area of older, inefficient, deteriorating housing, older factories, and abandoned buildings such as former warehouses. Because its status as a centre of lower-cost housing, it is especially attractive to people with lower incomes or who are new to the city — particularly new immigrants and often racialized minorities. This is a zone in transition because it is marked by transience with simultaneous inward and outward movement of residents. On one hand some people are moving in search of affordable housing in accessible areas of the city near to downtown. On the other hand, the upwardly mobile members of the working class are moving out as they become better off and seek newer and less deteriorated housing in neighbourhoods with more amenities such as parks, community centres, or newer schools. Transition, as occurs with the movement of people in and out of neighbourhoods leads to the breakdown of neighbourhood norms, traditions and infrastructures. This makes social regulation and moral education by group members and residents more difficult.

It is in the zone in transition that Park and Burgess locate the highest concentrations of crime. Their key thesis is that criminal activity is associated with areas that are experiencing disruption, turmoil, or disorganization.

The connection between social disorganization and crime and deviance is most fully developed in the works of later Chicago School researchers Clifford R. Shaw and Henry D. McKay. Shaw and McKay sought to illustrate the spatial distribution of crime by mapping occurrences over various time periods. They accepted and sought to show evidence for the claims of Park and Burgess that crime was concentrated in the inner city areas of the zones in transition. They further noted that crime rates declined as one moved out from the city core.

One of the central claims of social disorganization theories is that the failure of any community or neighbourhood to develop shared values and to organize collective ways of dealing with local problems, leads to a breakdown of effective means of social order or social control within the community or neighbourhood. With an incapacity or inability to act collectively comes individual expressions of frustration resulting in or expressing crime or deviance. Crime and deviance are actually normal or reasonable responses of normal or reasonable people to abnormal or unreasonable social contexts.

Shaw and McKay offer several primary claims to explain crime and deviance on the basis of social disorganization. First, they suggest that crime and deviance result from the breakdown or disappearance of local, direct, communal practices and informal social controls. People experiencing conditions of disorganization are not irrational, they are responding in understandable, even predictable ways, to the breakdown of communal and collective infrastructures. Second, the processes that give rise to disorganization and the breakdown of communal and collective infrastructures, and shared positive values, are not atypical or unusual within contemporary contexts. Rather they are the central ongoing processes that mark modernist societies: industrialization, urbanization, migration, and marketization of social life and necessary resources. Third, the distribution of residences and resources, and their positive characteristics, are the outcome of ecological processes, particularly competition and dominance. Those areas that are most desirable within the city are fought over and typically, within capitalist economies, conquered by economic and political elites. Fourth, areas of disorganization are marked by the transmission of cultural values that support deviance and crime as legitimate practices and which supplant values of conformity and adherence to mainstream values. Those values of conformity to mainstream norms and respect for laws are not transmitted from generation to generation within disorganized areas.

This last point reflects the notion of cultural transmission that becomes important within Chicago School theory. Cultural transmission suggests that norms, values, and beliefs are transmitted from generation to generation in informal networks, including families, work groups, gangs, and neighbourhood clubs. The more time one spends within a group, the more the values of the group are internalized. As one internalizes values of the group, one become resistant to the norms, values, and beliefs of others who are viewed as outsiders. Without communal and collective infrastructures to inculcate and encourage positive values, negative values as expressed in subcultural or reactionary groupings will become more feasible alternatives, over time, even becoming dominant.

In areas of disorganization, those adults who are most economically successful often achieve their success through deviant careers, such as drug dealing, pimping, gambling, or various underground economies. These, then, serve as attractive options for younger residents who see these careers as the best route to financial advantage. Thus, in turn, recruitment becomes easier. As more young residents are recruited, groups emerge, such as gangs, which form their own deviant norms, values, and beliefs. This development further marginalizes other norms, values, and beliefs that might serve as buffers or provide disincentives against crime. Thus, the cultures that are selected for transmission are those that are supportive of, and reinforce, deviant careers or criminal practices.

Notably, crime rates remained the same even if ethnic or cultural complexity changed. The same neighbourhoods showed the same deviance rates regardless of which ethnicities were present there over time. Shaw and McKay could claim, thus, that crime is rooted in the neighbourhood structure rather than the characteristic practices of specific ethnic or cultural groups. The detailed research of the Chicago School found that these criminality patterns were recorded in crime rates over a period of almost 70 years.

Building Community

The social ecology theories make clear that informal relationships, groupings, and activities, particularly face-to-face community interactions, exert as much or more influence on social behaviors as do formal or official institutions. In the absence of close, participatory networks and familiar relations of mutual aid and community solidarity to shape behavior crime is a likely, even predictable, outcome and response to social conditions. As Tönnies and Durkheim suggested, conditions of anonymity, impersonality, and instrumental relations without broadly shared community values can contribute to criminal activity. Social ecology theorists expand understanding by bringing the analysis closer to home, literally. Through their analysis one can see that the structuring of neighbourhoods can produce or heighten the experience of *anomie*.

The social ecology model is opposed to individualist explanations that suggest that criminals move to certain areas of the city. Rather, social ecology suggests that anyone experiencing such conditions of disruption, disorganization, and deprivation can be driven to resort to criminal activity to meet basic needs in an underserviced area, an area lacking fundamentally necessary resources. In addition, people in areas of disruption or turmoil are less likely to have access to social ties, or shared values and informal social control mechanisms, such as neighbourhood "eyes on the street." Furthermore, they might lack accepted or agreed upon local shaming practices that would serve to limit criminal activity.

Crime is the result of "normal" or regular folks inhabiting "abnormal" or irregular environments. Crime is not about pathological people. Although it might be about unhealthy environments or social settings. Anyone living under conditions of disorganization can be a likely participant in criminal activity.

Social ecology theories also counter the claims of Social Darwinism that poor cultures are unfit and thus deviant. Social ecology theories show that it is the structure of a neighbourhood that most influences criminal activity within it — not the presumed characteristics of the people who reside there.

One positive outcome of social ecology research has been the realization that collective action and community organization and mobilization — what might be called activism — can be, and usually is, more likely to lessen criminal activity than any formal punitive or regulatory apparatus like police forces or security guards. Social ecology research has encouraged the deployment of resources to support projects in socially disorganized or economically deprived neighbourhoods. The mobilization of resources for community centres, medical clinics, free schools, communal childcare, and collective laundries are all examples of activities that have helped people improve their quality of life, while lessening crime in specific neighbourhoods in which such efforts have been undertaken.

Projects such as InSite, the safe use drug centre in Vancouver, have shown positive results in improving community health while reducing harmful activities in the neighbourhoods around the centre. InSite is located in the poorest neighbourhood in Canada, the Downtown Eastside of Vancouver, an area that is lacking in formal resources but which has benefited from the collective efforts of a variety of local community activist groups.

Contemporary Social Ecology

Social Ecology theories continue to influence thinking about criminal activities and societal responses to crime. Since their origins in the 1910s and 1920s, they have been taken up and revised in light of changing urban development patterns and social policy initiatives. Indeed, social ecology theories have been particularly influential in shaping social policy and urban planning decisions.

In the 1960s and 1970s, social ecology was applied to address emerging struggles and conflicts, particularly the social uprisings and riots of the late 1960s. The National Commission on Civil Disorders, or Kerner Commission, in the U.S. concluded in its report that the riots and civil unrest in the U.S. during the mid and late 1960s resulted from the ongoing confluence of racist practices and policies within urban centres, both interpersonal and structural, and the economic inequality and worsening material conditions for sections of the working class, particularly among African Americans. Even more, the report highlighted the failures of government-initiated programs and policies, particularly around employment, housing, welfare, and education, to effectively address the needs of poor and working class residents of the cities. Frustration with social conditions, and the recognition that governments were unwilling or unable to improve conditions, encouraged outbursts of violence and removed restraints on engaging in riotous activities. The commission concluded that white racism against African Americans played significant parts, perhaps the significant part, in heightening frustrations and contributing to civil disturbances. Of significance remained racist attitudes among police forces in urban centres.

The commission recommended wide ranging transformations in the structure of urban centres. Part of this transformation should include thoroughgoing desegregation and diversification to end ghettoization. Governments should invest billions of dollars to end residential segregation and move away from public housing based in high density, high rise housing units and toward smaller scale and spatially diffuse settlements. The commission also encouraged government investment in job creation strategies and programs as well as funding for educational and training projects to address economic inequalities. The commission also suggested that government encourage the opening of closed suburban areas to African American residents while also supporting the movement of African American workers to emerging industrial centres outside the traditional cities.

Critics contend that the commission did not address fundamental structural inequalities and only served as a substitute for real social change. In such a view, the commission served to give government a surface appearance of concern and responsiveness while avoiding real policy initiatives that might have challenged local power holders. Even more, the commission served to reinforce law and order policies which only hindered more progressive, community-based, alternatives.

More recent works in social ecology have examined impacts of the physical environments in local areas on occurrences of criminality and perceptions of criminality, especially fear among residents. Researchers have examined effects of specific spatial arrangements and structures of the built environment on criminal activity. This is combined with renewed focus on processes and structures, formal and informal, of social regulation within specific sectors of the city, such as residential areas or commercial zones. As with early social ecology theories, there is an emphasis on uneven distributions of crime and the characteristics of neighbourhoods that affect the observed distribution patterns.

Emphasis on social disorganization continues to play a key conceptual part in contemporary theories, with both progressive and reactionary implications for communities. Negative consequences of recent approaches will be examined in a following section.

More recent work has echoed the analysis of the Kerner Commission in stressing the importance of the intersection of class and other forms of oppression, such as ethnicity, race, culture, in structuring crime in neighbourhoods. Ghettoization and poverty can contribute to isolation, frustration, and justifiable anger that can legitimize criminality as acceptable, even desirable or necessary, behavior. Research in a wide range of advanced capitalist contexts (Canada, U.S., Germany, Australia) shows that neighbourhoods experiencing multiple forms of exploitation and oppression (poverty and racialized inequality, for example) will be affected negatively in multiple ways. Government policies and housing programs, dictated and directed from above with little input from affected communities, can and do make these situations worse.

A recent extensive study in Ottawa, Ontario illustrated the intersection of poverty, racialization, crime, and vicitimization (DeKeseredy, Alvi, Schwartz, and Tomaszewski 2003). Using a victimization survey, the researchers outline experiences of crime and fear among residents of a low-income housing estate. They make suggestions for improvements in the estate that go beyond the limitations of the criminal justice system. Recommendations include improved housing conditions, labour market supports, access to better paying jobs, and improved public transit service to assist with work and child care responsibilities.

The concentration and segregation of poor and racialized groups in under resourced and economically deprived neighbourhoods leads to structural exclusion from established economic, political, and cultural venues, and encourages alternative means of social success or advancement and status achievement, including those that are criminalized.

Notably, recent studies suggest that the presence of crime in a neighbourhood is more significant than the socioeconomic status of the people who are present in the area. In other words, a lower income youth in a poor neighbourhood with high crime rates will be more likely to engage in crime than a person of similar status in a low-crime neighbourhood, even if it is an economically deprived neighbourhood.

In addition, recent studies suggest again that transition appears to be a key factor. Recent urban research suggests that areas experiencing gentrification and renewal, with new money and resources coming in with wealthier residents, also experience increases in crime rates (Taylor and Covington 1988). Part of this relates to the propensity of wealthier residents to regularly call police against poorer residents, homeless people, and sex trade workers in the area.

More recently researchers have examined the impact of neighbourhood structure and disorganization on residents' experiences of fear and perceived threat. Higher crime rates in disorganized areas can result in increased levels of fear and perceptions of threat as disorganization magnifies or exaggerates the threat posed by crime. Less impact is shown within neighbourhoods in organized and resourced areas, even for similar activities.

Fear circulates through stories of victimization that can be blown out of proportion or even become urban myths. This distortion of stories is made easier in contexts of anonymity where people may not directly know the people involved or what actually happened, and may only be hearing the story second or third hand from people they also do not know well, or through the mass media. The impact is that people become more withdrawn and secluded within their own homes. This self-imposed seclusion has a reinforcing effect, in that fewer people on the streets or in public spaces such as parks and walkways, can lead to increased crime as there are fewer "eyes on the street" to discourage criminality. This, in turn, creates more fear and results in increased seclusion. And on and on it goes.

Lack of community participation can lead to a decline of shared spaces and resources such as community centres and a withdrawal of local capital as businesses or services close or leave for other areas. Eventually, those who can leave, do, and transition increases, thus reinforcing, again, conditions for the breakdown of informal controls and increases in criminality.

High levels of fear can make people distrust or fear their neighbors and can lead to a weakening of already tenuous communal ties. Those infrastructures that do exist can become subjects of mistrust or skepticism. Community groups may be viewed unjustly as encouraging or excusing criminality, or acting for their own, rather than community, benefit.

Recent research shows that social disorganization and lack of communal networks and infrastructures also leaves communities with little political power and reduced capacity to make collective demands on governments and businesses to free up resources for community needs (Shantz 2010). The lack of political organization in community advocacy groups leaves the community disadvantaged both in absolute terms (according to their own real needs) and in relative terms, with reference to other communities in the city who are able to mobilize to make demands on civic leaders.

From Social Ecology to Social Reaction: From Defensible Space to Broken Windows

By the 1980s, and continuing since, wealthier residents and business owners mobilized for reductions in services for poor and working class communities, and called instead for tax cuts and grants to businesses and the economically privileged. The last thirty years have experienced what is referred to as a neoliberal phase of capitalist development in which classical liberal appeals to reduce or remove community control of private capital, and deregulate markets have taken hold politically. Neoliberalism presents an economic rationalist framework for dealing with social issues. Economic efficiency, and profitability, for capital is privileged above all else. The result has been a variety of programs of enforced austerity against the working class and poor, including cuts to social spending and programs that benefit non-elites, such as welfare, affordable housing, tuition freezes, and universal health care. There is a re-duction or removal of previously universal provisions for the disadvantaged. At the same time policymakers have been cutting social programs, they have provided tax cuts, grants, and subsidies to corporations and the wealthiest individuals and communities. It represents a massive transfer of wealth up-wards, away from poor and working class communities and into wealthier communities and businesses.

As economic hardships for non-elites grow, social welfare is replaced with law and order politics and increased spending on police and prisons. Neoliberal dis-courses construct contemporary society on the whole as being disordered and requiring surveillance, discipline, and punishment to restore order. Dangers of crime are exaggerated as a political justification for the extension of state au-thority, particularly against targeted groups, such as street youth, squeegee-ers, indigenous communities, and welfare recipients, who are selected for regula-tion and control. The rationale for this is the protection of private property.

In the neoliberal context of withdrawn community resources and cuts to social services, environmental approaches to criminology have returned to promi-nence. Forms of criminological theory focusing on neighbourhood character-istics have played a significant part in public discourses around criminality and especially around notions of crime control. These theories, rather than advocating communal and collective infrastructures and shared resources, such as community centres, childcare, or improved housing stock, call for in-creased social controls within specific, particularly lower income, neighbour-hoods. Even more, they target poor neighbourhoods, and the people of lower income who reside within them, especially homeless people, for surveillance, criminalization, and even removal. These theories call for a range of neigh-bourhood transformations, including restrictive barriers, surveillance mecha-nisms, and the presence of security personnel, to more rigidly control be-havior within neighbourhoods. Rather than calling for an increase in shared, communal, public spaces, these theories call for a closure of public spaces or, often severe restrictions on access to previously public spaces. The model of civic activity for these neoliberal criminological approaches is not the active citizenship of equals but the limited and unequal consumerism of taxpayers or ratepayers. The wealthy are encouraged to pay for privatized services while public social spending for necessities in poor and working class neighbour-hoods is drastically cut.

Conservative, neoliberal, criminologists have developed theories of crime prevention through urban design. Influenced by the work of criminologist C. Ray Jeffery and architect Oscar Newman in the 1970s, criminologists have claimed a relationship between physical space and crime rates. In his book *Defensible Space: Crime Prevention through Urban Design* (1972), Newman argues that there are noticeable variations between well-designed housing projects and poorly designed housing projects in terms of criminal activity, where other variables (population density, for example) are similar.

A key component in this perspective is the notion of defensible space — space that is controlled by residents. Defensible spaces are ones that residents feel comfortable using — so they maintain a regular, active presence there and are able to survey and assess their neighbourhood on a regular basis. Aspects can include physical barriers and increased lighting. Playgrounds, parks, and comfortable benches can encourage residents to be out, visible, and present in their neighbourhood, thus discouraging negative activities. The built environment, then, can remove or limit opportunities for criminal activity.

A dominant perspective within theories of environmental control, one that has become highly influential within government policy circles and been taken up by city governments from New York City to Toronto, is the "broken windows theory." The theory was introduced by conservative criminologists George Kelling and James Q. Wilson in the 1980s. The primary claim is that minor, perhaps nuisance, activities, such as panhandling, loitering, and gambling, or less managed neighbourhood features, such as abandoned vehicles and empty buildings, or unsavory spaces, such as XXX cinemas, will eventually lead to harmful and violent activities. These identified behaviors and spaces supposedly give a sense of neglect and lack of concern in a neighbourhood that will encourage criminal activity. Broken windows in buildings suggest to criminals that no one cares what goes on in the neighbourhood and no one will bother them. The response is harsh zero-tolerance policing that criminalizes activities that have not previously been targets of concern.

This theory is a central feature of neoliberal restructuring of urban policy and planning and has been used to justify a range of practices that have harmed poor and homeless people in various urban settings. In New York City under then mayor Rudolph Giuliani, homeless people were arrested, cleared out of the downtown core, and moved to warehouse shelters in the suburbs. This was a political practice that has been identified as "social cleansing," the targeted removal of poor and homeless people from city areas in an effort to make those areas more attractive for investors, business owners, and tourists. Similar social cleansing has occurred in Toronto and Vancouver after the introduction of broken windows-inspired "Safe Streets" acts that criminalize squeegeeing and panhandling.

Research consistently shows that there is minimal, if any support for the notion that broken windows policy has any positive effect in reducing crime. If anything, it is associated with acts of violence against homeless people as individuals take it upon themselves to "clean up the streets." In New York, broken windows policies were associated with increases in instances of police brutality, particularly against members of racialized groups (Goff 2004).

These theories again harken back to classical theories by emphasizing rational choice as a primary factor in criminality. These contemporary theorists argue that people make rational calculations that weigh costs and benefits before engaging in any act. Environmental design attempts to make clear that success in criminal or deviant activity is not likely and the costs of engaging in crime actually will outweigh the benefits — especially by raising the likelihood of surveillance and the risk of being caught. The overall effect is to give the appearance of a community that cares and is actively involved in the upkeep and maintenance of the community and community spaces.

In addition to those already mentioned, there are a number of serious problems with these neoliberal theories of spatial control. Governments following these approaches take resources that could be used elsewhere and put them into surveillance of areas and activities that might never have led to crime in the first place. There is a sense that crime is simply waiting to happen but no evidence for this.

These approaches also lead to expressions of insularity and xenophobia (fear of others) as people who are not part of the neighbourhood are treated as criminal "others" or as illegitimate. This can increase a sense of isolation and play into "us versus them" sentiments that increase conflict and lead to greater problems for a city, including racism and poor bashing violence against poor and homeless people.

The construction of "good" and "bad" people often emerges on the basis of stereotyping along lines of race, class, sexuality, culture, or status (including citizenship status). It can even lead to the violent targeting of people who are not a criminal threat. Vigilante violence and killings of homeless people, as have occurred in Toronto and Vancouver recently, provide examples of how this can have fatal consequences.

Another serious, if often overlooked, outcome has been the privatization of social development in urban centres. Wealthier people and neighbourhoods rely on private security and surveillance systems, thus calling for reductions in funding for shared public resources that might otherwise be distributed on the basis of community need. This plays into neoliberal market policies that cut social spending in favor of tax breaks to the wealthy and no-tolerance policing of poor neighbourhoods. Wealthy, resourced communities end up with greater resources while poorer, under resourced communities are left with even fewer resources, even as real need in the community might be increasing.

Conclusion

Social ecology theories, apart from neoliberal theories, have helped to shift analysis away from the individual level and have drawn attention to the structural factors within neighbourhoods that can contribute to deprivation, social problems, and crime. Still there remain a number of problems with social ecology theories.

First, they accept state definitions of crime as well as state practices for targeting crime within specific communities. The identification of high crime areas, as in Chicago School research, is based on the use of police records alone. Yet these records do not show where crime is actually happening, they only show where policing is happening. Arrest records reflect police surveillance rather than actual occurrences of behavior. A related result is that social ecology theories assume that working class neighbourhoods are most prone to crime. They almost entirely define crime as street crime.

Second, crimes occur outside of disorganized areas but may not be sought after by authorities. Much elite crime, such as fraud, insider trading, illegal dumping, or exploitation, is occurring in wealthier, suburban areas yet it is not detected and does not lead to arrest because police cannot access the neighbourhoods in question, which may be private, gated communities intolerant of being subjected to surveillance by police.

Third, ecology theories cannot explain why the vast majority of poor people, even in disorganized areas, do not engage in criminal activity. Social ecology theories cannot explain why specific crimes occur or why most people choose not to engage in criminal activity despite experiencing great deprivation and frustration.

Fourth, they assume that resources will be made available to assist disorganized areas. They overlook that fact that economic and political elites will resist the allocation of resources to poorer neighbourhoods and will fight to ensure that resources are transferred to meet their own interests. They are aided in this by having greater access to local politicians and by having more recognized political resources at their disposal.

Fifth, the social ecology theories assume that poorer neighbourhoods are disorganized. Research suggests that there is much informal organization within poor neighbourhoods, including in community advocacy groups and social movements. There are often more expressions of solidarity and reliance on mutual aid in poorer communities than in wealthier ones. Wealthier communities are often more anonymous and detached.

Finally, social ecology theories do not even follow their own logic. If transition and turnover are key contributors to crime, then one would not look first or only to inner city areas. One would look to the area of transition and turnover *par excellence*. That area is obviously the suburbs. By definition, suburban areas are new areas with few shared traditions, values, or norms. They might only be years, rather than decades, old. They are areas of rapid population movement, inward and outward. They are also areas of anonymity and indifference. Yet suburbs tend to be higher income than inner city neighbourhoods and thus, the social ecology theories overlooked them.

Other sociological theorists have attempted to examine the ways in which social processes create definitions of criminality and pursue various forms of punishment. They seek to explain how certain groups or communities come to be targeted for surveillance and state intervention while others are overlooked. Issues of power and the control of ideas — who gets to assign blame and who benefits — are central within such perspectives. These theories are examined next.

CHAPTER 7

Learning and Labelling: Social Relations Theories

Social relationship or social learning theories hold that criminal behaviors are learned in interaction with others, particularly but not exclusively, those within close personal circles such as family, friends, and neighbours. Criminality is not inborn, biological or genetic. It is not limited to people of specific backgrounds, resources, or opportunities. All people have the potential to engage in criminal or deviant acts regardless of social standing. Criminality is a function of the socialization process. Thus, social relationship and social learning theories focus on interactions or socializing processes between individuals, often in a close face-to-face context. Unlike social structural theories, which as macro-structural theories emphasize large-scale, often abstract, social structures and institutions, such as the economy, labour market, education, government or culture; social relationship theories tend to be micro-structural, focusing on relationships within specific, immediate, settings or locations. Where structural theories speak of labour markets and unemployment, social learning theories will examine relationships within specific workplaces or between individuals and the unemployment office. While meso level theories, such as the social ecology theories examined in the previous chapter, will look at the neighbourhood as a primary area of focus, social relationship theories might look at interactions within specific community groups.

Social relations theories challenge notions of social consensus that suggest that acts are criminalized on the basis of broad social agreement. While consensus models overlook real differences in how behaviors are defined and addressed, social relations theories view understandings about crime and deviance as shaped by a variety of social factors. Social relations theories reject absolutist claims about crime and punishment, arguing instead that definitions of criminality and deviance are contested, and suggesting that perspectives on crime and punishment are related to the social positions and backgrounds of those who do the defining. Notions of crime and deviance are the outcomes of disagreements and debates around which there are very many differences of opinion and values.

Rather than taking for granted the definitions of crime and deviance provided and pursued by authorities as mere reflections of reality, social relations theorists suggest that what we take as the reality of crime and deviance is actually produced socially. Crime and deviance are socially constructed. One person's crime is another person's "business as usual." The crime of one is not necessarily treated the same as the crime of another, particularly in societies in which the distributions of power, resources, and authority are vastly unequal.

This also raises the question of who gets to do the defining, of who gets to label someone as criminal. Thus, social relations theories are attuned to the importance of studying and understanding the importance of power relations within stratified societies. In order to understand crime, we must study social interactions, both among those who engage in activities that become criminalized and between those who define acts as criminal and those who are defined as such.

Social Interaction and Social Relations Theories

As is the case for the middle range social ecology theories, it is also the case that social relations theories are rooted in the works of theorists of the Chicago School of sociology. In particular, social relations theories find early expression in the social psychology approach of Chicago School theorists. Social relations, learning, and labelling theories are influenced by sociological and psychological theories of symbolic interactionism as expressed in the works of Charles Cooley, George Herbert Mead, and Herbert Blumer. Symbols, the collective sharing of symbols, and the interpretation of symbols, are central to these theories of social behavior. Symbols are simply objects or practices that represent, or stand in, something else. Language is symbolic. Art is symbolic. So too are body movements, gestures or facial expressions. In order to operate in society, we all must learn to read accurately and respond effectively to the symbols around us. Sometimes symbols are unclear or ambiguous and we must improvise or innovate our responses on the basis of "best guesses" or predictions. Symbolic processing is not a passive practice. We do not simply receive pre-established symbols. We also actively and creatively shape, define, revise, refresh, and interpret those symbols. Meaning creation and the construction of definitions are interactive processes.

A key concept in symbolic interaction is role playing. This is a part of all social development and it allows people to take on the role of the other, to see the world through other peoples' eyes. Understanding how symbols are received provides insights into meaning and meaning creation. Interaction is only possible if people are able to interpret adequately the meaning expressed in the symbols offered by the other. Definitions — and the sharing of definitions — are key.

The meanings of signs and symbols are constructed through collective practice. These are active processes and meanings can be challenged, contested, or revised. We collectively construct reality and definitions of reality through the wielding of symbols. A symbol that no one else recognized would be socially meaningless. Make up your own language — then speak it to others. They will wonder why you are speaking nonsense and probably respond symbolically by giving you a frown or raised eyebrow.

Not only external symbols, but our overall sense of self is constructed collectively through social and symbolic interaction. Notably we internalize the symbolic gestures of others, incorporating them into our own sense of self. The works of Cooley and Mead have given rise to a notion of the looking glass self. Your sense of yourself is a reflection of how you are viewed by others, and how you perceive yourself to be reflected in their interactions with you.

According to symbolic interactionism, people interpret symbolic gestures from others and incorporate them into their own self image. For example, if someone frowns or sneers at you, you will wonder what the trouble is. Have you done something wrong? Is there something on your shirt? Is your fly open? What if they flip you the bird or stick out a tongue at you? Thus, negative reactions, whether verbal or expressed in body language, could cause a person to view themselves in a negative light. Your "self concept" may be disturbed or troubled and you may be left with self doubt.

A key concept is the self-fulfilling prophecy. People can begin to act out the way they are perceived even if that perception was initially quite inaccurate and even if they themselves believe that the perception is untrue. If enough negative symbols are directed your way, you may develop a negative sense of self, even against your own better judgments.

Context is crucial in the construction of definitions and responses. The same circumstance can elicit different definitions and responses. Did you do well on the test because you worked hard and studied or because the test was too easy or because of the good work of the instructor? Did you do poorly because you did not keep up with your notes or because the instructor was unclear?

Definitions do not always reflect actual situations or what might be called "reality." What is crucial is how people interpret events. Those interpretations may be factually incorrect but still dominate perspectives of reality. This is true of medieval views of the Earth as the centre of the universe, as discussed earlier. It also describes public misconceptions about crime. People often perceive crime rates as increasing even as they are decreasing. The public also perceives street crime to be the most frequent and harmful crimes when in reality elite crimes are likely as frequent and certainly more harmful.

These insights would provide a central part of labelling theory which would look at the effect of social signals, given by teachers, police and other justice officials, and media upon adoption of criminal identities. All of this shows that meaning is collectively constructed. It is a social endeavor. But in stratified societies not one in which all participants are able to participate equally. Not everyone is able to apply their definitions in specific contexts and only some are able to make their definitions of a situation stick broadly or publicly.

Social Learning Theories

Social learning theories of crime and deviance find their most influential early expression in the work of University of Chicago sociologist Edwin Sutherland's "differential association theory" of the 1930s. For Sutherland, crime is a function of learning that can influence anyone in any culture. Notably, Sutherland avoided the tendency of most of his peers to focus on working class subcultures or crimes of the poor. Sutherland's work was groundbreaking in focusing attention on professional and corporate crimes, at a time when few did, and it was, in fact, Sutherland who coined the term "white collar crime." To understand the learning of crime, Sutherland examined the recruitment and socialization behaviors of elites within their exclusive institutions, including corporate offices, private clubs, professional schools.

Differential association theory suggests that close and trusted relatives and companions teach criminal behavior and attitudes, creating and sustaining a context in which the emphasis on supporting crime outweighs the emphasis on opposing it. Significantly differential association theory examines not only the learning of deviant acts, specific techniques or skills, from influential peers. Even more, it notes the ways in which peer networks teach people to deal with criminality psychologically. Close and trusted friends, relatives, and associates teach criminal attitudes as well as behaviors. Thus, peers teach people to rationalize or legitimize their activities helping people to shift from rule-abiding to rule-breaking identities in a way that supports their deviant or criminal choices. They create a climate or environment in which the emphasis supporting crime outweighs the emphasis against it. Corporate criminals rationalize their activities as "only doing business" or "helping the economy," for example. Youth deviants justify their acts as "being cool" or "not being square" or "flipping off authority." In such learning environments and relationships, people learn specific deviant acts, but they also learn to justify those acts. This can involve a desocialization of previously internalized inhibitions against crime. It also involves resocialization in favor of crime.

Social learning theories have been prominent within social psychology since the 1970s. Social psychologist Albert Bandura's social learning theory emphasizes modeling and the processes by which people learn not only through direct experience but also by observing others who they respect or admire. Role models in the media, arts, sports or music can influence people to act in desirable or undesirable ways. Bandura notes that observation of violent acts, as on television, could be reflected in violent acts by child observers.

Labelling Theories

The most significant social learning theories of crime are labelling theories, which, following the work of Howard Becker, examine the development of criminal careers from a first act of, possibly harmless, deviance, rather than the causes of crime itself. A key question for labelling theorists asks how some acts come to be defined as criminal or deviant, with the people who commit the act being punished, while other, even more harmful, acts go without notice or consequence. Labelling theories transform thinking about crime and deviance placing emphasis on the role of authorities in defining and targeting acts and individuals as criminal. For theorists like Becker, crime and deviance are the outcomes of social processes involving competing definitions, and differential capacities to define and impose rewards and punishments for specific behaviors in society. For labelling theorists crime is not a matter of violating a social consensus about the rightness and wrongness of an action but rather about the ability of some groups in society to have their own interests presented as consensus. Definitions of crime and deviance are contextually constructed and not all are able to participate equally. Notions of consensus are, in fact, outcome of social processes of power.

Labelling theories emerged and became prominent within sociology and criminology during a period of great social and cultural contestation during the 1960s and 1970s. This was a period in which the perceived social consensus of the 1950s was shown to be a social myth as various groups, particularly of those excluded from or unhappy with their role and place in the 1950s "consensus," began to challenge and confront openly the assumptions of social agreement around issues of gender, race, sexuality, and culture more broadly. Movements, and the collective actions of women, racialized minorities, indigenous people, gays and lesbians, and the poor called into question the basis of perceived consensus which privileged wealthy, white males and offered alternative perspectives on society, history, and politics. The social movements of the excluded and exploited, and the struggles that they engaged, revealed the "American Dream" to be a fiction for much of the population and showed that there was no social consensus. Social reality was very much a matter of social conflict, disagreement, and debate.

The formal beginnings of labelling theory date to the early works of Franklin Tannenbaum in the 1930s, particularly *Crime and Community* (1938). Tannenbaum points out that many forms of juvenile delinquency are simply normal parts of adolescent street life. They are part of the play, experiment adventure and excitement that form crucial parts of individual and social development. To others, particularly outsiders of different age cohorts, such activities may be seen as threatening or a nuisance and they may demand the intervention of some form of social control or punishment, whether through police or school officials. Such intervention begins a process of change in the manner in which the targeted individuals and their activities are perceived and treated. There is a gradual shift from the definition of specific acts as evil to the re-defining of the individual him or herself as evil. Everything about the individual, friends, clothing, speech, music and so on, is turned into an object of scrutiny and evidence for a delinquent nature. For Tannenbaum, individuals thus targeted may eventually learn to view *themselves* as delinquents. This process Tannenbaum refers to as the "dramatization of evil" as the child or youth is separated out of its group and subjected to negative treatment. Not only criminals are made deviant in this manner, but others who simply violate norms or conventions rather than laws, particularly members of youth subcultures. Tannenbaum noted that the poor are more likely than the wealthy to get caught up in this process. This point has been developed by critical criminologists and conflict theorists.

Building upon these insights, labelling theory attempts to examine the social and interpersonal processes through which acts, attributes, and beliefs come to be constructed as deviant. It attempts to explain how cultural and individual perceptions create and sustain deviant identities. For labelling theories, deviance results from the enforcement of rules rather than specific acts. The deviant person is simply someone to whom the label "deviant" has been successfully applied, not someone who is fundamentally different. Even more they are people who have come to believe the label as it applies to them.

A central text in the development of labelling theory, and one of the most influential texts in criminology, is Howard Becker's work from 1963, *Outsiders: Studies in the Sociology of Deviance*. Becker engages in ethnographic participant observation, directly involving himself in subcultural venues, to understand jazz musician subcultures and activities like marijuana use. Through his work, Becker outlines processes of "becoming deviant." Deviant identities are not ready made. Becoming deviant involves sequences of steps that lead the individual to commit to a deviant identity and to participate in deviant careers.

Notably, Becker identifies and outlines the important part played by people outside the subcultural circles, particularly authority figures, in creating and assigning deviant identities or labels. These people who are not part of the particular subculture mobilize to target the subcultural group and its members for moral condemnation and legal punishment or criminalization. These people are termed by Becker as moral entrepreneurs. They are people who strive to chastise the behaviors of others, often for their own benefit or profit.

Examples of moral entrepreneurs are shopkeepers who call police on homeless people or urge politicians to pass laws like the "Safe Streets Act," not because they are concerned about homeless people but because they are worried that the presence of homeless people near their shop might hurt business. Other examples include people who mobilized for the prohibition of alcohol in the 1920s or current campaigns against marijuana use. The moral entrepreneurs engage in moral enterprises. These are efforts, campaigning or lobbying for example, of an interest group to codify in law prohibitions against activities that perhaps only the moral entrepreneurs themselves view as morally wrong. Moral entrepreneurs are usually among the economically and politically privileged members of society who have some connections with mass media in publicizing their concerns and with politicians in passing legislation.

A key aspect of labelling theory is the impact of interactions within the criminal justice system on people who have been identified and labelled as deviants or criminals. Labelling theorists note that most people have engaged in deviant, even criminal, acts but do not consider themselves to be criminals because those events pass without notice or regard. However, if someone is caught in such an act a process is engaged that shifts the person's self perception. Being arrested, identified, brought to trial, and perhaps jailed is what labelling theorists call a "degradation ceremony," in which the person subjected to it is initiated into a deviant role and assigned a deviant label. In this way, criminal justice systems are actually massive deviance-producing machines. Within their operations people are taken into the system and converted into deviants — they are given new deviant identities that they did not previously bear. This is the identity they carry with them publicly.

This process often alters a person's self concept as well as disrupting personal relationships and changing life chances and opportunities, including negatively impacting employment, housing, and education. To be publicly defined as deviant is to carry an expectation that you will behave in certain ways. By assigning negative identities, conforming members of society, and those with the power to assign labels, strongly influence offenders' future behavior. One outcome is the internalization of the label of deviant or criminal by the person who has been processed through the system. Particularly, the person may take on the role that the label signifies. People learn to adopt behaviors and attitudes consistent with the label. Someone defined as deviant or criminal may come to play out activities associated with such labelled roles.

Labelling has negative social and psychological consequences for people. Stigma is the term used by Erving Goffman (1963) to refer to the mark of disgrace that is associated with deviant or criminal labels. Stigma shapes how others view the labelled person but also shapes how they see themselves. Goffman analyzed how people who are positioned within devalued roles struggle against these positions, often times throughout the rest of their lives.

A significant impact is that negatively labelled people can become segregated from non-labelled people or non-offenders. Thus, they turn to others who have likewise been labelled and associate with them. They may find camaraderie among those who have been labelled and not have access to others who have avoided labelling. This can set the stage for the establishment of deviant or criminal subcultures or groups.

Labelling theorist Charles Lemert makes the distinction between primary and secondary deviance and suggests that the first is connected with the second through labelling. Primary deviance refers to the initial act of deviance or law breaking. It may be an immediate response to an immediate problem as when someone steals a loaf of bread because they are hungry or cheats on an exam because they could not study properly. It may be intended as a "one off" event. They may feel guilty and intend it as their last offence. Everyone engages in acts of primary deviance. But if you are caught and labelled, it may lead to what Lemert calls secondary deviance. Secondary deviance is the response to a label. It occurs when one assumes the deviant role or a deviant identity.

People are turned into deviants through official procedures that are about the exercise of power and authority within stratified societies rather than strictly expressions of justice. Labelling theories challenge notions of social consensus that propose social order as resulting from broadly agreed upon goals and values. For social relations theorists reality is socially constructed or produced through the activities of disparate and varying groups both internally and through their interactions with other, more or less powerful, groups. They stress the importance of power relations within a given society and suggest that it is essential to know who assumes the authority to do the labelling in society. This will help to explain while less harmful acts, such as shoplifting or squeegeeing, often carried out by less powerful members of society, are targeted for criminalization, and the deployment of criminal justice system resources, while more harmful acts such as pollution, product safety or unfair labour practices, acts undertaken by corporate elites, are less likely to leave the perpetrator with a deviant or criminal label. Similarly labelling theorists might suggest that schoolyard bullying receives proportionally more public attention than a variety of corporate crimes. Even more, elites who might be labelled have greater resources available to fend off or overturn a label. They will be less negatively impacted by a deviant label if one is applied.

For labelling theorists, the negative consequences of labelling must inform criminal justice system policy. These consequences can be more negative and broadly harmful for society than the activity that led to criminal justice system intervention in the first place. Stigmatization can initiate social processes that lead to criminal careers in response to activities that might have been fleeting or regretted otherwise. Thus, the criminal justice system should avoid intervention and labelling processes, particularly for lesser "offences." Arrest, publication, court appearances, and detention should not be initiated for low level activities according to labelling theorists. Victimless activities or non-violent actions, such as pot use, squatting, or sex work, should not be criminalized — or should be decriminalized. A more tolerant and non-invasive approach should be taken and there should be opportunities for diversion from the more stigmatizing aspects of the system throughout. Restorative justice and peacemaking approaches can offer important alternatives here.

Labelling theorists emphasize that some people have the power to make their labels stick while others cannot. The definition of deviance or crime is a form of social control exerted by more powerful actors over less powerful actors. Labelling is part of a process that excludes subordinate actors from social participation or from power.

Control Theory

During the 1970s and 1980s, conservative versions of social relations theories emerged that found support among neoliberal policy makers seeking to regulate society, and especially poor and working class members of society, broadly on the basis of a uniform, singular, authoritarian moral vision for society as a whole. Such theories would gain prominence from the 1980s through to the present. These conservative theories are known as control theory or social control theory. The theories affirm the connections between the individual and society — they are in that sense sociological. But they approach these connections in an absolutist manner emphasizing traditional notions of discipline, authority, legalism, and social regulation.

The most influential version of control theory is offered by Travis Hirschi in a range of works produced over the last 40 years. Hirschi starts from the premise that all people are by nature (harkening back to biological positivism) anti-social "risk takers" who will commit crime if given the opportunity. Hirschi views people as egocentric and self-serving (like market actors, once again). In his view, people seek to satisfy their desires following the easiest path available — including criminal pathways (O'Grady 2007, 81). The only restraints on people are the bonds they have with society which raise the costs of risk taking to unacceptable levels. Thus, Hirschi's theory draws upon classical theory and appeals to notions of rational calculation in human behavior. It is the image of the market involved capitalist trader transposed onto all of human behavior. Such a view served suitable for economic and political elites seeking to impose neoliberal, capital friendly policies for regulating contemporary societies.

Control theory contends that if a person is adequately bonded to society, they will not likely pursue crime. Where bonds are underdeveloped, broken, or strained, then individuals will pursue their egocentric drives and commit crime or engage in deviant activities (O'Grady 2007, 81). The role of society, for Hirschi, is simply one of control and regulation of individuals (rather than mutual aid, solidarity, or care). This again betrays a neoliberal view of human social life.

For Hirschi and control theory there are four primary social bonds — commitment, belief, attachment, and involvement. These reflect "inner controls" and "outer controls" on the individual. The combination and strength of bonds will determine whether conventional means or deviant ones will be pursued, especially for young people, according to Hirschi and control theory. The two inner controls are commitment and belief. Commitment refers to the investment — in time and emotions — that one has in conventional or conforming activities such as school or work. One committed to success in university and getting a degree will avoid criminal behavior since it could jeopardize those goals, according to control theory. The second inner bond, belief, refers to one's adherence to dominant values, moral systems, and legal procedures or laws. Violating one's beliefs will, for Hirschi, elicit in the individual a deeply felt sense of guilt or regret (O'Grady 2007, 83).

The first outer control is attachment. This refers to one's emotional connection and affinity for those individuals and groups that are in one's life. If a person has a strong attachment to their parents, they will not want to embarrass or hurt them through commission of illegal activities according to control theory. If the attachment is weak, they may not be inhibited by what their parents might think or feel. Attachment can work to make a person more empathetic or sensitive to the feelings of others.

The final bond, the outer bond of involvement, speaks to activities and behavior patterns that shape opportunities that are present for individuals. Hirschi claims that engaging in conventional activities like sports or school and after school clubs will reduce opportunities for individuals to engage in criminal acts and will weaken the psychological support for such acts.

Control theory has been influential in social policy circles, particularly over the last thirty years. It has encouraged the initiation of school programs and after school programs as well as family training to encourage families to teach acceptance of conventional values and institutions. Often these programs have involved funding and direction from private, for-profit organizations and businesses rather than being publicly delivered. This has raised concerns about corporate control over school environments and activities and community-based programs. It has also provided motivation for police-school liaisons and school visits by authorities. This has raised additional concerns about the stealth policing, and increased policing of poor and working class communities, and criminalization of their members, under the guise of "building bonds" with the community.

Despite the policy influence that control theories have had, there is little evidence that control theory has any real explanatory power beyond minimal forms of deviance undertaken by some youth. This reflects important problems and gaps in the theories. First, strong bonds will not discourage crime if the bonds are with family members, peers or groups that are engaged in or supportive of crime. Strong bonds with youth gangs or family members engaged in crime will not impede criminal involvement.

Second, there is little evidence that engagement in supposedly conventional activities like sports will deter criminality. In some cases such participation may, in fact, encourage criminality or provide cover for criminality. Some sports teams may provide "walls of silence" to protect deviant members, as in certain sexual assault cases involving athletes. Similarly the team may be a source of deviant or criminal activity such as the use of performance enhancing drugs or violent hazing rituals for rookies or new recruits (O'Grady 2007, 83).

Third, Hirschi's control theories show their bias against the working class and poor. They focus, once again, on street crimes (drug use and gang activity, for example) but not on elite crimes of any sort. Indeed, economic and political elites often have the strongest and most secure bonds with conventional values and institutions. These very bonds may facilitate the engagement of elites in crime and deviance, as when corporate lawyers and accountants work to cover up illegal corporate activity or use close personal networks to lobby politicians to remove regulations or to "look the other way" on corporate wrongdoing.

Differential association shows that close networks, and strong interpersonal connections, provide the learning centres for crime. Thus, tight knit groups can be incubators of crime. Notably Sutherland and differential association theories suggest that conventional, or even admired, groups can provide the support for criminal activities or criminal careers as when students in business school learn means to circumvent regulatory agencies and oversight.

Indeed, control theory, in its various formulations, fails to analyze issues of power, class, gender, racialization, and inequality. Such an analysis is the real task of sociology. Control theory does not live up to its sociological require-ments. It assumes a shared "human nature" based on egocentrism and pursuit of self interest, and it fails to recognize that these are dominant characteristics, not of all humans but of capital. Control theory is unable to account for the structural and social conditions that reinforce egocentrism as favored features, not of humanity but of a specific type of society. It is exactly this question, of the social contexts for understanding behavior, which must be addressed by sociological theory.

On the whole, control theory shifts attention away from structures of power, inequality, exploitation, and oppression in society. Instead it places emphasis on the family and supposed problems of socialization within the family. It reinforces broad prejudices that crime is a working class issue and is related to the incapacity of working class families to socialize their children properly.

Thus, control theory plays into, and has supported, neoliberal policies that condemn supposed "cultures of poverty" and blame, for example, single mothers or absent fathers for youth crime. The effect of such approaches is to reinforce biases that assign blame unfairly and further burden peoples' attempts to care for themselves and their families in difficult circumstances. The actual impact of this is to make situations worse for people who already face disproportionate obstacles and barriers. Conventional institutions, thus, rather than being part of a solution are part of the problem. They serve to legitimize or justify relations of inequality and injustice and punish those lacking resources in society while letting elite wrongdoers off the hook.

Conclusion

Crime and criminality are part of broader, ongoing, and active social processes. These processes are generative of, and generated by, relations and practices of power. This suggests that crime and criminality, and our understandings of them, are not objective. They are constructed, and chosen, by actors within criminal justice systems who have the power to define certain acts and people as deviant or criminal.

Social relations and social learning theories are significant in showing that societies' definitions determine whether or not behavior is deviant or criminal and these change over time and place. Often these definitions are the outcome of social struggle, inequality, and exploitation. Furthermore, labelling theory shows that labelling, and the activities of schools, police, criminal justice systems, media, and prisons may actually perpetuate crime rather than reducing it.

CHAPTER 8

Capitalism and Crime: Critical Theories

Critical theories have their roots in radical political movements such as Marxism and anarchism. Since the 1960s, influence has come from feminist and anti-racist movements as well as post-structuralism and anti-imperialist theories. These theories make important contributions to understandings of crime and punishment in contemporary capitalist societies. They also offer important beginnings for envisioning alternatives.

Critical theorists argue that the roots of modern crime problems are linked with those of modern capitalist economies. Capitalist societies, founded on a broad division of labour and highly stratified with vast disparities of wealth and poverty, are grounded in often sharp conflicts. A system based on economic inequality, capitalism is marked, and has been throughout its history, by profound struggles over social resources and political decision-making. A central conflict occurs between those who own and control property and resources, the bourgeoisie or capital, and those who have to sell their labour in order to survive, the proletariat or working class. Extreme differences between "haves" and "have-nots" give rise not only to conflict but to sociopolitical institutions that serve to regulate that conflict, typically in ways that secure the success of elites and dominant classes. For critical theorists, the criminal justice system is a mechanism for elite social control and the preservation of economic inequalities to maintain elites' interests.

The post-war period, following World War II, promised growing social prosperity. Working people sacrificed much to defeat fascism and totalitarian governments in Europe and Asia. They had been induced to put their lives on the line with the promise that they were fighting to defend and expand democracy. Upon their return from battle, they made demands for increased political and economic democracy in their home contexts. Yet they were confronted with growing differences between haves and have-nots in society, as well as discrimination on the basis of gender, sexuality, racism, and status. They were confronted by the contradictions between political systems that promised and lauded democracy at the same time as smashing dissent and criminalizing protests, as during the period of civil rights demonstrations. The social protests of the late 1960s and early 1970s showed the breakdown of the supposed social consensus claimed by conservative commentators. Growing waves of rebellion and social movements raised the consciousness of disparate people about the social inequality of modern capitalist societies. Issues of racism, patriarchy, class, homophobia, environmental destruction, war, and imperialism motivated millions of people to organize to change society for the better.

Newly active groups of young people, including university and college students were drawn to, and played major parts in, the emergent movements. These youth took their experiences of community organizing and community struggle into their classrooms and asked why the mainstream theories did not explain their social experiences and the problems in the world around them. They challenged instructors and demanded new theories that offered better, more accurate, explanations of the society, which questioned rather than reinforced power relations. They drew upon theories that circulated in the community movements they were part of. These theories were critical of unequal and exploitative social structures and relations. The students and youth turned to theories that analyzed politics and economics to understand crime and deviance. They identified the acts of elites as criminal and deviant, and contested the role of states and the police who were arresting them simply for standing up for what they knew to be right. That attempted to silence them. Thus, critical theories emerged or became more prominent within social science disciplines like sociology and criminology. Figures like Stanley Cohen, Jock Young, Carol Smart, Stuart Hall, and Ian Taylor would be influential parts of these movements in criminology.

Consensus for Whom? Hegemony and the Manufacture of Consent

Critical theories are often contrasted with "consensus theories" that suggest that the basis for society is social consensus, an unspoken general agreement, on broad social issues. For critical theorists, notions of consensus serve to cover up or diminish inequalities and relationships of power that determine, or at least condition, the social opportunities, capacities for decision-making, and positive action within people's lives. Consensus suggests that decisions made by powerful and influential members of society, those individuals and groups that have resources to impel social development in a way that benefits their interests, are willfully accepted or agreed to by those lacking power. Where non-elites contest or challenge inequality, they are often met with criminalization, oppression, or repression.

In fact, for critical theorists this is not consensus, but more akin to fear or compulsion. In this manner, elites are able to assert their very particular interests as the interests of society as a whole, largely because opposition is marginalized or silenced. This construction of particular elite interests as "common interests" is a process that some conflict theorists term hegemony. Drawn from the writings of Italian Marxist Antonio Gramsci, hegemony refers to the manner in which dominant groups are able to condition non-elites to accept their subordinate status. Media theorist Noam Chomsky modifies this concept to speak of the "manufacture of consent" as elites are able, largely through mass media but also through schools, to secure and maintain the capacity to govern over subordinate groups. For critical theorists, consensus theories of crime and deviance serve this process of hegemony by deflecting attention away from social structures of inequality and power, that might be opposed and changed, and toward the failings of individuals who are responded to with punishment or medicalization.

Critical theorists prefer to focus on elite deviance, involving acts that are socially, economically, and ecologically harmful rather than on minor street crimes and the nuisance activities and survival strategies of the poor.

Critical theories argue that the state administers largely to capitalist interests. Agencies of government target not only the underclass but the working class as a whole. Working class crime is more visible, whether school crime or street crime. In addition, working class people lack access to necessary resources to get away with "invisible crimes," such as fraud, tax evasion, insider trading, or influence peddling.

Capitalist ideology even conditions the very ways in which crime is perceived, i.e. largely in terms of an ethic of individualism that separates the understanding of social problems from their social structural contexts of inequality and power. Individuals, presented abstractly without reference to specific histories and experiences, are blamed for acts and attention is diverted from the socioeconomic structures in which the acts take place and are perceived. Institutions within capitalist societies, such as government, media, the police and courts, tend to individualize highly complex issues and depoliticize the emergence of deviant activities by referring such activities back to "damaged" or deviant individuals who are in need of treatment or punishment. Indeed, for conflict theorists, the very notion of "the individual" is a recent modernist notion. This is part of hegemony and the manufacture of consent.

Powerful groups are able to mobilize public opinion on behalf of their interests. The law is itself created by economic elites who control the production and distribution of major resources in society, including intellectual and educational resources. Legislators are influenced by powerful segments of society through lobbying groups, political action committees, and campaign contributions.

Dominant groups shape public perceptions of crime and its definition. Focus is shifted to "street crimes" and the crimes of working class youth, such as drug use, petty theft, shoplifting, and minor assault, rather than corporate crimes or government crimes; the crimes of elites. Dominant institutions also create "worthy" and "unworthy" victims of crime. Affluent victims receive more press coverage and minority and low-income lawbreakers are more likely to be publicized as criminals than are corporate leaders, whose crimes may actually be more harmful to individuals, society, and the environment.

For critical theorists, authorities should not be assumed to be acting on behalf of society at large, but for their own interests and on behalf of other dominant actors. Laws, rather than expressions of general will or social contract, are methods for a privileged group to oppress or exploit an underprivileged one. Laws against theft, squeegeeing, or squatting prevent a redistribution of social wealth — a relevant point given that most crimes are actually property crimes.

Critical theories emphasize that some people and groups wield power and are able to make their definitions of situations stick, while others lack this

Chapter 8: Capitalism and Crime: Critical Theories

capacity. The definition of deviance is a form of social control exerted typically by more powerful actors over less powerful actors. Within this process, authorities (the dominant) learn norms and practices of domination while subordinates (subjects) learn norms and practices of deference.

Critical theorists do not take rules and regulations as given but rather view them as part of a sociopolitical process. Labelling of crime and criminals is part of a process of conflict which excludes subordinate actors, particularly poor and working class youth, from social participation or from power. It can marginalize those who challenge or reject the status quo that leaves them in positions of unequal status.

The key factor is relative power. Within capitalist societies, the poor have the least power and thus, we might expect them to have the highest rates of criminalization; which is not to say that they exhibit the highest rates of deviance or crime. This helps to explain, for conflict theorists, why in North America poor, Native, African-American youth are the most criminalized, given the most negative attention by the state.

Critical theorists argue that contemporary criminalization processes work to ensure that those who are brought within the criminal justice system are typically of the lowest socioeconomic standing. Deviants, in a society that demands material accumulation, are those who are not succeeding and/or do not accept their diminished status. The poor are more likely to be arrested, formally charged, go to trial, be convicted, and receive harsher sentences. Poor communities are often treated by government and police as though they are enemy territories subjected to sustained and intrusive surveillance.

For critical theorists, working class youth within capitalist divisions of labour are socialized, from early ages, to accept subordinate positions within society, including unsatisfactory labour within jobs that offer little satisfaction and few opportunities for personal growth and advancement. Without that socialization, which is a necessary part of the process of hegemony, working class youth would rebel and pose a challenge to the inequalities of the status quo social relations and their place within them. Numerous studies from within conflict perspectives, including the work of Peter McLaren and Paul Willis, explain the ways in which public schools are structured to prepare working class youth for manual labour. Part of his preparation includes the targeting and punishment of recalcitrant youth who rebel against the bleak prospects their futures are deemed to hold. Working class youth subcultures become markers for resistance against the apparent gap between the promise of upward mobility and the reality that this is beyond their reach. In the face of this rebellion, instituted authorities wield formal rules and laws and informal moral discourses to reintegrate working class youth within dominant structures of inequality.

Crime, Capitalism, and Power

Critical theorists argue that labels of deviance and criminality, and the application of labels, have special associations with people who impede or obstruct the operations of capitalism. Such labels are less often, even rarely, applied to those who benefit from capitalism.

There are several specific reasons for this association. First, because capitalism is founded upon, and maintained through, private ownership and control of productive forces; those who threaten private ownership are regular candidates for labelling as deviant or criminal. These can include poor people who steal or shoplift, or union organizers who seek increased wages. At the same time, landlords who charge poor tenants exorbitant rents for unsafe housing and/or evict those who cannot pay rent on time, are not considered anti-social or a public threat to society, despite the actual harm they might cause. They are allowed to continue with harmful activities under the excuse that they are "only doing business." After the Second World War, German war criminals were forbidden from using the excuse that they were "only following orders"—"only doing business" is the contemporary version, and it is regularly accepted as an excuse.

Second, because capitalism depends on productive labour, the labour of working people, for profit, those who cannot or will not provide their labour power for capital risk being labelled as deviant or criminal. It is very telling, and reveals much about the real purpose of criminal justice systems in capitalist societies, that from the very beginning of modern, liberal democratic justice systems, laws have been devised and implemented that target unemployed, poor, and homeless people simply because they are unemployed, poor, and/ or homeless.

In order to maintain ideological dominance and gain acceptance for great social inequality, capital requires cultivated respect for approved authorities.

This may be the economic authority of capital, in asserting a right to own and control the majority of social wealth. It may also be the political authority of politicians or the legal authority of judges. These are constructed authorities that are imposed on the basis of power. Acceptance of these authorities is an outcome of power and must always be refreshed and defended by powerful groups who benefit from the acceptance of these economic, political, and legal authorities. Thus, those who resist such imposed authorities, by organizing alternative political movements or by breaking laws, are typically labelled as deviant or criminal. Workplace and community organizers will often be labelled as troublemakers or malcontents.

Finally, it can be said that anyone who threatens, directly or indirectly, the economic, political, and/or legal status quo, runs the risk of being targeted for labelling, and repression. This can include labour organizers and trade unionists, environmentalists, feminists, and anti-racist activists. It can also include critical criminologists who contest dominant views of social, economic, and political authority.

On the other hand, in contradistinction to the way in which those who impede capitalism are treated, society provides positive and beneficial portrayals to those who facilitate and enhance the operations of capitalism. Star athletes, regardless of real contributions to society, become constructed as heroes and role models and are provided numerous opportunities as spokespeople. One reason they are favored is that they express or represent values of competition and individual reward that are vital to ideological depictions of capitalism.

The history of criminal justice systems and laws within capitalist societies and liberal democratic governments, is replete with examples of the criminalization and punishment of unemployed, homeless, and poor people. Vest resources have been devoted simply to punish and chastise the poor and unemployed merely for being poor and unemployed.

So-called vagrants, the unemployed and homeless, have been regularly targeted for criminalization and medicalization within liberal democratic polities. In the early period of capitalist development, in England the New Poor Laws of 1834, supported by newly enfranchised capital, gave government authority to arrest unemployed, poor, and homeless people and place them in workhouses. There the emphasis was on forcing people to labour. Conditions in the workhouses were unsafe and inhumane. Notably there were no "Rich

Laws" that forced capital to put wealth to socially beneficial use. Versions of poor laws exist today in the form of Safe Streets Acts that criminalize homeless people and allow the state to detain them. Other contemporary practices, such as workfare, involve state legislation to force people to work for capital in order to receive welfare benefits or social assistance.

The work of Michel Foucault has examined the history of factories and workhouses, public schools, prisons, and military barracks as sites for the discipline of the poor and working classes, and as spaces where they have been instructed to accept their station as workers. Foucault discusses the emergence of the Hôpital Général in France during the nineteenth century. The hospital was initially used to house all and any who could not or would not work. Among those so designated were beggars, vagabonds, the poor, ill, unemployed, and thieves. The purpose, and sole excuse for detaining them was to instill work discipline. The hospital represented a fear and distrust of idleness among the emergent capitalist class or bourgeoisie. The hospital and the detention of poor and unemployed served the interests of the merchants, business, and landowners who required a vast pool of cheap and compliant labour free from rights to organize and bargain their labour price. It also provided a mechanism to remove so-called troublemakers or nuisances, such as community and labour organizers and social reformers. As capitalism developed, over time the ruling classes segregated those who could work from those who could not since the latter were disrupting the reserve army of labour. Those who could not work were labelled insane and dealt with through specialized practices. This was instrumental in the rise of psychology. Thus, the psychological professions emerged as a result of state and economic interests to control and regulate labour. Mental health experts found that they could make a tidy living providing services to capital. Similar practices exist today as psychology is used to increase the productivity of labour for capital.

The class character of criminal justice systems in capitalist societies is also clear if one looks at the emergence of policing. Modern policing, as deployed in liberal democracies, emerged in the seventeenth and eighteenth centuries to regulate the growing working class and poor populations of people who had drifted into urban centres after being forced from their communal lands through various processes of enclosure and privatization of what had traditionally been the commons. These former peasants found themselves in crowded, dirty, unhealthy living environments in the slums of factory cities. And they were upset about it. The wealthy, rather than address the concerns

Chapter 8: Capitalism and Crime: Critical Theories

of the poor, preferred to observe and regulate them. The new capitalist classes of business people and property owners viewed the poor and working classes as "dangerous classes" who needed to be made subservient to capital. Policing emerged as part of the regulatory and punitive regimes for disciplining the urban poor and working classes of the growing city centres. Indeed, the very name of the police comes from the Greek word *polis*, meaning the city.

The first modern police force was founded under King Louis XIV in 1667 as an attempt to regulate the city of Paris, the largest city in Europe at the time and the one considered most dangerous to the wealthy. The royal edict of March 15, 1667, that instituted the police is quite telling. It gave police the task of "ensuring the peace and quiet of the public and of private individuals [capital], purging the city of what may cause disturbances [reformers], procuring abundance [private profit], and having each and everyone live according to their station and their duties." The last part makes it apparent. The police should ensure that everyone live according to their station or class and carry out their assigned duties — to work to create value for capital. The police were developed to ensure the maintenance of class inequality, exploitation, and social hierarchies.

The first modern police forces in the U.S. were developed in industrialized urban centres in the industrialized northeast. Their main emphasis was "maintaining urban order" in the face of class conflict as cities grew through waves of migrants seeking employment. In American history, numerous cases show that local business people have had influence, even control, over directing police against striking workers. The earliest forms of policing in the southern U.S. involved so-called "slave patrols" dating back to 1712 in South Carolina. The function of these patrols was to maintain discipline over slaves and prevent slave riots. Black people caught violating any laws were summarily punished.

State forces were formed to deal with striking workers. The Coal and Iron Police were created in Pennsylvania in 1866 to control striking coal and iron workers. In 1905 the state formed a state police agency for use in strikebreaking. These official state forces gave a legitimacy to strikebreaking that private security, which lacked state authorization as keepers of the public order, could not claim.

These purposes are reflected in the present with the policing of protests and demonstrations against economic injustice. The period of alternative globalization protests has seen a number a dramatic clashes between police and protesters. The protests against the WTO in Seattle in November 1999 gained the nickname "The Battle in Seattle." Demonstrations in Quebec City (2001), Genoa (2001), Miami (2003) and London (2009) have seen running street battles between demonstrators and police. The Genoa and London protests also saw the death of civilians due to police actions.

The overall aim of these laws and practices is to force people to sell their labour, to work making profits for capital. These laws and policies are really about imposing work discipline and upholding the power, authority, and privilege of capital. Working people, the proletariat, are compelled to accept their status and work for wages for an employer. Understanding this is crucial to understanding crime, punishment, and criminal justice systems in capitalist societies.

The Greatest Theft: Exploitation and Value

Understanding crime and punishment within capitalist societies requires an understanding of value and exploitation. Critical theorists make a distinction between use value (the quality or uses to which a product can be made) and exchange value (the quantitative measure of what one can get for something in trade). People produce things because they have some kind of use for them; they meet some need or desire. This is where the qualitative aspect of production comes in. Generally people prefer products that are well-made, function as planned, are not poisonous, and so on. Under capitalism, exchange value, in which a coat can get two pairs of shoes, predominates use value. This is the quantitative aspect of value that does not care whether the product is durable, shoddy, or toxic as long as it secures its (potential) value in sale or other exchange with something else.

And capitalism's driving focus on the quantitative at the expense of the qualitative also comes to dominate human labour. The quality (skill, pleasure, creativity) of the particular work that people do is not primarily relevant for the capitalist (except that skilled labour costs more to produce and carries more exchange value). That's partly because exchange is based on the quantity of "average-socially-necessary-labour-time" embodied in the product human labour produces. That simply means that if some firm takes a longer time to produce something on outdated machinery, they can't claim the extra labour time they take, due to inefficiencies, compared to a firm that produces more quickly using updated technology (and that's one reason why outmoded producers go under).

Capitalist production is geared toward exchange as the only way that surplus value is actually realized rather than being potential; the capitalist can't bank surplus as value until the product has been exchanged. Use value plays a part only to the extent that something has to have some use for people or else they would not buy it; well, if the thing seems totally useless, the bosses still have advertising to convince people otherwise. Under other non-capitalist "modes of production," such as feudalism, most production is geared toward use value production rather than exchange value.

Surely if people are producing to meet their needs, they will continue to produce use values (and even a surplus of them in case of emergency) without regard for exchange value. Certainly people would value their work (qualitatively) in ways that cannot be imagined now since they would be meeting their community's needs and would try to do so with some joy and pleasure in work, providing decent products without fouling up the environment.

Under such a system, labour, the capacity for creative production, also becomes a commodity. Indeed, for the poor, dispossessed, and working classes, labour is the only commodity that they possess by which they can meet their survival needs. Lacking capital, and ownership of productive wealth, members of the working classes must sell their labour commodity — their capacity to work — in order to survive. The commodity labour is sold on a labour market, like any other commodity would be sold in a capitalist society. Looking for a job is simply taking your labour commodity to the labour market. You hope to make a sale to capital (the purchasers of labour) — to get a job. If successful, you are employed. You made a sale. There are others, possibly millions, on the labour market competing against you to sell their labour commodity. If you are unsuccessful on the labour market in this competition, you have failed to make a sale and are now labelled as unemployed. This is viewed as a personal failure in capitalist societies rather than a normal, regular, everyday outcome of labour market competition and exchange.

Even more, the labour market is unequal and imbalanced. The purchasers — capital — have far more power than the sellers — labour. There are fewer of them and they control the market. If one worker wants more for the labour commodity than capital wants to pay, capital can go elsewhere to the hundreds of others who might have applied for the job. Some will be willing to take less because without pay they cannot feed, house, or clothe themselves. Sellers of labour are desperate in a system in which they do not own land or resources and can only rely on the sale of their labour in order to survive. Capital has the luxury of waiting for a deal they like. Labour has no such luxury. Failure to sell one's labour — the condition of unemployment — could prove fatal. Thus, despite representations of the capitalist market as based on competition, it is really only competition among the sellers of labour. Capital runs a near monopoly over the market and the purchase of labour. This imbalance, and the greatly disproportionate power of capital, marks all relations in capitalist societies favoring the owners and controllers of capital over those who have only their labour by which to survive.

If you are lucky enough to make a sale on the labour market, your exchange value is met in the form of a wage, payment for labour. The level of exchange paid by capital is simply enough to keep you coming back to work, no more, no less. Not paying enough would lead you to return to the labour market to seek a new deal, and that would raise the costs of labour for capital by having to pay recruitment fees or train your replacement. Paying you too much would cut into profits, not at all desirable for capital, so the impetus is always to pay you as little as necessary to keep you around. The price you can exact for your labour is variable, depending on the value it represents. If you have added value to your labour, by getting a degree or through training or serving as an apprentice, you might expect, or require, a higher price in the exchange for your labour. The labour that has gone into your commodity may increase its value. It will take more to keep you coming back to work. Your costs will have gone up and that will be reflected in what you seek and accept at the labour market.

Now you have a job. You have made a successful sale of your labour on the labour market. At this point, you are about to be subjected to what critical theorists consider to be the greatest theft in capitalist societies. It is a theft that is massive and which takes place each and every day of your working life. Yet no one is criminalized, arrested, or punished for it.

Capitalist ideology depicts the market as a realm of freedom and equity. According to this depiction, buyers and sellers meet and mingle to exchange goods in a way that is mutually beneficial and need is traded equally for need.

Chapter 8: Capitalism and Crime: Critical Theories

One side has too many apples and needs oranges, another side has too many oranges and needs apples. An equitable trade ensues to meet the needs of each side. So, if this is true, your wage should reflect exactly the value you produce for capital. Capital needs your labour in order to make the product — they cannot build it alone. You need the wage, in the form of money, which you can use to buy food or pay the rent. So if you sell your labour for $40, your workday should end when you have produced $40 of value in product for capital. That would be a fair and equitable exchange. Value for value. At each point during the working day or week, you produce enough in value to pay for yourself. You produce the value for capital reflected in your wage. That point should mark the end of your work day or work week. Yet it does not. Go ahead, calculate the point at which your labour has paid for its wage and leave work. Capital has wielded, over generations, political and legislative power to force you to work long after the point at which your labour has created value equal to your wage. You might pay for your daily wage after two hours of work, in the value you generated in product, but still have to work another six hours. This is a massive theft, a freebie for capital. You are having six hours of labour and six hours of your life stolen from you. If you are paid $40 per day, but produce $40 in value after two hours ($20 per hour) and are forced to work another six hours, you will, by the end of the day have seen $120 of value that you have produced taken from you and kept by capital every working day. Multiply this over the course of your lifetime. Multiply it by the number of other workers in your workplace. This is an enormous theft that is global and generational in scale, billions of dollars taken from working people and their communities and controlled by capital. This theft is called surplus value, the extra value workers produce that is stolen from them by their employers. It is what critical theorists define as exploitation — the economic theft of labour time and value by capital. Yet the criminal justice system does nothing to stop it. In fact, it supports and sustains it. Instead of theft, it is called, in an ideological cover up, "profit." Profit sounds much nicer than theft. Go ahead and call the police and tell them you have been robbed at work. You will be the one arrested, not your boss.

The fact that surplus value and exploitation, the theft of labour time and value by capital, is not criminalized tells you all you need to know about the class character of criminal justice systems and law within capitalist societies. The theft represented by surplus value in your lifetime exceeds the theft of all of your possessions (car, stereo, television, home, and so on) combined. And nothing is done about it. If someone robbed you of $100, you would be out-raged. Yet millions of dollars are stolen from you, and the theft occurs every day of your working life, and nothing is done about it, no questions are asked. Talk about concern for crime by governments rings hollow given that the theft by exploitation not only goes unpunished by governments but is, in fact, sup-ported and justified by governments in property laws and labour regulations.

This is the myth of the market as a mechanism for fair exchange and human freedom. The capitalist market does not, in fact, work this way. In reality, the market is marked by inequality and power imbalances. Monopolies are able to wield overwhelming force in the market and can force unfair and harmful deals on individuals who are desperate and lack alternatives.

Understanding Intersectionality: Feminism and Critical Race Theory

Within capitalist societies, class-based experiences of exploitation are always connected with specific forms of oppression and deprivation on the basis of systemic and structural inequalities related to social identity within stratified social relations. These include processes of racialization, patriarchy, sexual prejudice, and age bias. Critical theorists refer to these connections and rela-tionships of exploitation and multiple forms of oppression as intersectional-ity. That is, forms of exploitation, oppression, and inequality intersect with each other. Working classes are not monolithic, they are marked by differ-ences of gender, sexuality, racialization, ethnicity, and culture. Where one ex-periences oppression along a single line of identity, as a woman for example, the experience is bad enough. When various forms of oppression intersect, as for a lesbian woman of color, the impacts of these oppressive conditions can multiply exponentially. For critical theorists, these various forms of oppres-sion, and their intersections, must be properly addressed in understanding criminality and, especially, regimes of punishment.

Feminist theory in criminology goes beyond class analysis to ask about the specific features of class and exploitation within capitalist societies. Feminist criminologists ask who holds and wields resources in society. The answer is overwhelmingly men. How, then, are women structurally disadvantaged within such relationships?

There are variations of feminist theory ranging from liberal to socialist to radical. Liberal theories, like other mainstream theories, do not question existing structures of power and authority. They primarily seek to limit or end women's disadvantage within those structures. Thus, liberal feminism calls for reduced discrimination or sexism against women and seeks to achieve greater representation of women within positions of authority. Attempts to increase the employment of women as police officers or as judges or politicians are aspects of liberal perspectives on feminist criminology. These are not critical approaches. Other feminists have attempted to move beyond liberal perspectives to develop critical theories in feminist criminology.

Socialist feminism notes that capitalist society values people on the basis of the paid work that they do, as discussed above. Women have historically been restricted or excluded from certain forms of employment or work in certain sectors. Notions of "women's work" have limited labour market opportunities for women and driven down the value of their labour. Socialist feminism asks why gendered roles are assigned to women in the first place and who benefits from such assignations. In addition, women usually provide socially necessary and important labour, such as child rearing or elder care for which they are not paid. This represents a massive devaluing, even theft, of women's labour.

Socialist feminists note that gender and sexual oppression is related to economic dependence on men. Women are doubly exploited and oppressed for their labour as well as sexually. They note that most women are arrested for property crimes, like shoplifting, or for sexual activities, such as prostitution. Indeed, if one takes a historical view, women have typically been criminalized for those activities that allow them a certain degree of autonomy in their labour, and which offer opportunities for independence from men. Activities such as witchcraft, which simply involved medicinal and herbal knowledge shared among women, was targeted and led to the murder of countless women. Simply for their knowledge, which benefitted their communities but threatened the power of male authorities. Similarly, abortion has been a medical service traditionally provided by women which has been criminalized. Another example of a health practice traditionally provided by women that has been criminalized is midwifery, the practice of experienced women, often elders, assisting other women in the birth of their children. All of these activities have been carried out primarily by women and have provided women some autonomy and social power — and all have been criminalized.

Against liberal feminist theories, socialist feminism suggests that increased job integration for women without adequate childcare or homecare will only lead to more work for women and more stress. This dual work pressure between employment outside the home and work within the home is referred to as a double burden. It reflects the double day that women are forced to work in jobs and at home.

Radical feminists focus on the systems of structured inequality that specifically oppress women. These structures constitute what is called patriarchy, which refers to systems of male domination that affect all women (though not in the same ways). For radical feminists, women are treated socially as the property of men. In Canada, for example, women were viewed legally as the property of their husbands until 1969 and husbands could not be charged with raping their wives until 1983. Radical feminists note that people who are structurally and socially unequal, cannot be made equal through laws and punishment as liberal feminists suggest. Rather than primarily seeking state measures or calling upon authorities to enact policy changes, radical feminists have worked to organize women in grassroots social movements to bring about social change through their own efforts and by creating and maintaining their own institutions and spaces. While radical feminists have managed to change obscenity laws and rape laws, they have also played important parts in the creation and sustaining of shelters for abused women and women's centres on university campuses.

In addition to gender and sexuality, another key aspect of intersectionality involves racialization. Critical race theory has addressed the connections between racialization, racism, crime, and punishment. Critical race theory argues that race and crime and their meanings are socially constructed. Social processes shape how people are treated and how crime is defined. Some groups are presented and being prone to committing crimes and are linked to particular crimes by criminal justice authorities and mass media.

Race is not biologically founded, as has been discussed earlier. Racialization denotes a social process, a process of power. Critical race theorists point out that racialization refers to a cultural process by which differences of appearance are made to stand as biological properties of "race." Race is, in fact, discursively constructed and can be applied to many different definitions depending on context. Nineteenth century scientific attempts to catalogue humanity by racial types linger in contemporary notions of race. While race is mythical;

Chapter 8: Capitalism and Crime: Critical Theories

racism, and acts of violence and prejudice associated with it, is very much real and is experienced as such by people subjected to it.

Stuart Hall argues that the use of classification, as by race, is a system of power. It is power written on the body or what some call biopower. Classification opens the door to other things such as ranking, and classification is also an ordering system that places some above others. In this way, society is further divided into different groups of unequal social standing.

For critical race theorists, criminal justice system practices have been bound up with racialization and racism. Racial profiling, for example, relies on stereotypes, rather than actual behaviors, to single people out for scrutiny (Shantz 2011). If black people are investigated more often and more regularly, there is a greater likelihood that police will find something eventually. Numerous studies in Canada have found that racism is a regular feature throughout the criminal justice system. Visible minorities feel over-policed and under-protected (Henry and Tator 2009). The victims of crime in racialized groups are left more vulnerable. Social status and age can insulate some groups from contact with police but this is not the case for black people in places like Canada and the U.S.

The universal legal being of classical theory is almost always constructed as a male white being who must be integrated into the market system. The law erases real social differences and overlooks the power inflicted by social processes such as racialization and racism. A gap exists between formal rights, which all are said to possess, and substantive rights that are not distributed evenly or equally in capitalist societies. Critical race theorists argue that the law must be rooted culturally and historically. Slavery, it must be remembered, was legal. It was supported and sustained by supposedly fair, neutral, and legitimate legal systems. So too were residential schools that destroyed indigenous communities and contributed to cultural genocide in Canada.

Systemic racism must be addressed through structural changes. Arguing for new rights is not enough.

Restorative Justice and Peacemaking Criminology

Critical theorists also reject disciplinary and punitive short-term approaches, such as police, prisons and penalty, via the state. Instead they emphasize restorative justice and reconciliation via community-based processes such as healing circles — a process that brings victims, offenders, and community members together to seek mutual understanding and restore social relations.

Restorative justice, while a relatively recent, and still somewhat marginal, component of modern criminal justice systems, has long been part of efforts to respond to and prevent crime within a variety of local communities. Approaches in criminology, such as restorative justice and peacemaking criminology, express the value of collective efficacy or "social capital," in which strong community networks of social support and informal social control contribute to reducing occurrences of crime. Restorative justice emphasizes effective practices for dealing with crime, based on consensual, interactive and participatory, rather than more familiar adversarial models of justice, based on retribution and punishment, that make up the overwhelming part of criminal justice system practice.

Proponents of restorative justice note that punishment-centred models of crime control are both ineffective and costly, both in human and resource terms. Prisons are wildly expensive systems for containing and managing people who have been targeted for criminalization, but, even more, incarceration has long been shown to offer few positive or constructive outcomes for those who are so punished. Advocates of restorative justice note that harsh prison sentences, at most, provide victims of crime with a sense of revenge or vindication. Punishment models do little to assist or support victims who may have experienced multiple impacts by a criminal event or events. Systems oriented primarily toward punishing offenders offer little to those who have been victimized by crime.

Restorative justice is concerned with rebuilding relationships after an offence, rather than driving a wedge between offenders and the community as occurs within criminal justice systems in capitalist liberal democracies. Restorative justice allows victims, offenders, and the community to address the harms done by crime, such that the community, rather than being further torn apart and pitted against itself, might be repaired. Rather than imposing decisions about winners and losers in an adversarial system, restorative justice seeks to facilitate dialogue among those affected. All parties with a stake in the offence come together to deal collectively with it.

Restorative justice acts on a range of general principles. First is the view that both victim and the community have been harmed by an offender's actions and this causes a disequilibrium that must be addressed to restore relations, lest more social harm be done. Counter to traditional criminal justice system approaches, offenders as well as victims and the community have a stake in a successful outcome of this process. Second, those who have offended have some obligation to address the harm they have caused. Third, restorative justice emphasizes the healing of both victim and offender. Victims need information, understanding, safety, and social support. Unlike the standard criminal justice system, offenders' needs must also be addressed, including social security, health care, possible treatment for addictions or counseling.

While conventional criminal justice focuses on the offence to the state by individuals and does little to deal with the consequences to the community and its members, restorative justice emphasizes rebuilding community trust and "social capital" as means to defend against future conflicts and offences. As Brennan (2003, 2008) suggests: "Restorative justice builds on social capital because it decentralizes the offense from merely the act of an offender breaking the law, to a breach in a community's trust in its members. This in turn allows the community along with the offender and victim to *collectively* look for a resolution."

One particular approach to restorative justice is drawn from the practice of indigenous sentencing circles. Within these healing circles, a broad range of community members are involved in the justice process to reintegrate offenders into the community rather than pursue the segregation model of the penal approach. Unlike adversarial processes as are practiced within the court system, sentencing circles seek solutions to the original conflict and possible underlying causes while working cooperatively to repair relationships harmed by the criminal act. Sentencing circles have been adopted within the criminal justice system in Canada as one option available to members of indigenous communities.

Peacemaking criminology argues that the idea of making war on crime needs to be replaced with the idea of making peace on crime. Bracewell identifies the motivating themes of peacemaking criminology as follows: "(1) connectedness to each other and to our environment and the need for reconciliation; (2) caring for each other in a nurturing way as a primary objective in corrections; and (3) mindfulness, meaning the cultivation of inner peace" (Lanier and Henry 2004, 330). This approach emphasizes the responsibilities that members of society have as active participants in maintaining and restoring positive social relations. Like other versions of restorative justice, it calls upon community members to address issues of crime and community health and safety directly through their own involvement rather than deferring to the power of instituted authorities.

Restorative justice is no utopian wish. In fact, it as been attempted within several jurisdictions to deal even with extremely violent crimes. Research suggests that restorative justice shows clear effectiveness, both in terms of offender accountability and victim healing (Umbreit, Coates, Vos, and Brown 2002).

Instead of escalating the violence in an already violent society by treating violence and conflict with state violence and conflict, through police and penal sanctions, society needs to de-escalate violence. Practices of conciliation, mediation, and dispute settlement become preferable options. Peacemaking criminologists, like anarchist-influenced Hal Pepinsky, argue that reducing violence requires people's direct involvement in democratic practices. By this he means "a genuine participation by all in life decisions that is only achievable in a decentralized, nonhierarchical social structure" (Lanier and Henry 2004, 330).

Providing community support for offenders benefits all in the community as well as representing fairness in the practice of justice. Restorative justice offers the prospect of escaping the "zero-sum game" of the traditional criminal justice system, whereby what is said to benefit victims must hurt offenders. In restorative justice, victim, community, and offender all stand to gain in their own ways.

CHAPTER 9

Homelessness, Criminalization, and the Right to Shelter

The Nobel Prize winning novelist and poet Anatole France was famously quipped: "The law, in its majestic equality, forbids rich and poor alike to sleep under bridges, to beg in the streets, and to steal their bread." A pointed commentary on the inherent inequality of laws that target the survival strategies of the poor and homeless (since the wealthy do not need to sleep under bridges), France's words have taken on heightened significance in Canada recently. Over the last decade in cities across Canada, those who have need to sleep in parks and other public spaces have increasingly experienced the "majestic equality" of the law against sleeping outside.

Policies such as the "Safe Streets" Acts in B.C. and Ontario have outlawed squeegeeing, or cleaning car windshields for money, and "aggressive" panhandling (while leaving police much discretion to determine what constitutes aggressive). In Vancouver, Project Civil City prohibits sleeping outside and has empowered so-called "Downtown Ambassadors," individuals hired typically by Business Improvement Areas (BIAs), in specific neighbourhoods of the city to stop, question, and compel homeless people to leave the area. In the lead up to the 2010 Winter Olympic Games, anti-poverty advocates, including the Pivot Legal Society, raised concerns that police were targeting homeless people for increased ticketing in areas such as Vancouver's Downtown Eastside, as a way to push them out of the area in preparation for the Olympics. In July 2008, Pivot Legal and the Vancouver Area Network of Drug Users filed a complaint with the B.C. Human Rights Tribunal claiming a violation of the rights of street people to use public space by the Downtown Ambassadors. On July

9, 2009 they received notice from the Tribunal that they had successfully opposed an application by the Downtown Vancouver BIA to dismiss the human rights complaint. A hearing is expected to proceed on that case. A recently released report of February 2011, confirmed the concerns of anti-poverty activists that poor people, youth in particular were targeted for removal from specific neighbourhoods before and during the 2010 Olympics.

For critics, policies and laws such as the Street Ambassadors program and Safe Streets Acts, constitute a growing criminalization of poverty in Canada. For some, these policies and practices constitute what Vancouver anti-poverty advocate Jean Swanson calls "poor bashing," the violation of people's rights simply because they are poor.

Homelessness: From Rights to Criminalization

Decent housing is viewed as a basic human right and recognized as such in the United Nations Declaration of Human Rights. For most of human history, housing has been part of community membership and even non-elites have had claim to some form of basic housing. This has changed with the development of economies based on market exchange and profit. Homelessness has been a regular characteristic of life within capitalist social systems as housing is made into a commodity like any other and people are required to pay rent on their dwelling or purchase their residence.

Homelessness has become a growing problem within wealthier industrialized countries during the last three decades, the so-called period of neo-liberalism or neo-liberal capitalism (Burt 1992). Neo-liberalism represents a conservative or New Right ideological approach to social policy in which programs, such as welfare, social housing, rent controls, and shelters, that primarily benefit the poor and working classes are cancelled or de-funded in favour of programs, such as tax cuts and corporate grants, that exclusively benefit the wealthy and socially privileged. During the neo-liberal period governments, in countries like Britain, Canada, and the U.S., have systematically cancelled key provisions of the welfare state. One result has been a growth in homelessness as people are left with fewer means to afford housing, and fewer options for lower cost or subsidized housing (Burt 1992). Unemployment, relating to workplace closures and the shift to a service sector economy during the neo-liberal period, has also left large numbers of the working classes in more precarious economic conditions. At the same time governments have responded to the problems created by social service cuts through an increased emphasis on punitive measures to contain and control growing ranks of the poor. This has meant not only increases in police and prison spending, but a range of legislation directed at criminalizing the poor and homeless.

Homeless people, particularly the street homeless, have been targets of violence, both interpersonal as well as legislative. In cities like Toronto, there have been numerous cases of physical attacks on homeless people by vigilantes, including the killing of a homeless man by armed forces reservists. Each year several homeless people die as a result of the lack of shelter. Governments, particularly municipal and state or provincial governments have contributed to moral panics around homelessness by publicly associating homelessness with criminal activity (O'Grady 2007).

The history of criminal punishment targeting homeless people shows the class character of governments, policing, and legislation, even within liberal democracies such as Canada. More recently, legislation has focused on the survival strategies by which homeless people sustain themselves on the streets. This includes prohibitions against public display of possessions to punitive legislation that bans panhandling and squeegeeing car windshields for money.

With the increases in homelessness in urban and suburban areas across the wealthier, industrialized countries, particularly during the neo-liberal period of the last three decades, there has come a corresponding increase in the practice and visibility of panhandling and other survival strategies of the street homeless. At the same time neo-liberal governments have preferred to cut or cancel social services, such as welfare, subsidized housing, and health care services, that benefit homeless people while simultaneously emphasizing criminal justice system approaches that police, regulate, and punish homeless people for engaging in survival activities such as panhandling. The result has been a proliferation of legislation prohibiting and regulating panhandling. In some cases, panhandling can result in jail time for the person involved.

Various anti-panhandling laws prohibit panhandling in a broad range of contexts and practices. While laws differ, certain prohibitions can be found across cases. These include prohibitions against: panhandling near ATM machines or bank entrances, approaching people in motor vehicles, following people or making repeated requests, panhandling outside stores or restaurants, panhandling in groups, using a loud voice, and panhandling while camping out. Clearly the prohibitions greatly restrict panhandling practices making it difficult for any panhandling to be carried out at all.

Criminalizing Homelessness in Toronto

In the late 1990s, during a period of high unemployment, growing homelessness, and severe government cuts to social programs; the conservative provincial government in Ontario, with much prodding from conservative representatives on Toronto City council, motivated for changes to the Ontario Highway Act to make squeegeeing and so-called "aggressive" panhandling illegal. The Ontario Safe Streets Act was finally established in January 2000. The resulting legislation makes it illegal to give "any reasonable citizen cause for concern." The law is a provincial statute, outside the federal jurisdiction of the Canadian criminal code. Yet, it provides police within the province with the capacity to ticket anyone believed to be engaged in squeegeeing of car windshields or panhandling "aggressively." It also prohibits street solicitation and hitch hiking. Homeless advocates argue that in sentiment and in practice this law has given police, local vigilantes, and business improvement associations great leeway to continue or expand the harassment of the poor and homeless.

The implementation of the Safe Streets Act in Ontario followed a period of moral panic over panhandling and squeegeeing in which high level politicians played important parts in stoking public fear and condemnation of people engaged in such activities. Toronto Mayor Mel Lastman publicly described panhandlers as aggressive "thugs." Adding to this chorus, the Ontario Crime Commissioner (charged with overseeing crime policy for the entire province) declared in an interview with the Canadian Broadcasting Corporation (CBC) that squeegee-ers and panhandlers were the province's top concern. In 1999, Mayor Lastman and the City Council launched a so-called Community Action Policing (CAP) program backed by $2 million of public funds. The program was designed specifically the allow police to "sweep" public parks and designated areas of Toronto in which panhandling was carried out and arrest or remove people.

The constitutionality of the Safe Streets Act has been challenged in the courts and the legitimacy of the Act contested in the streets through protests and demonstrations. A challenge, by people ticketed under the Act, that the law violated the Canadian Charter of Rights and Freedoms was unsuccessful in 2001. In 2007 the Safe Streets Act was again upheld by the Ontario Court of Appeal. Opponents of anti-panhandling legislation argue that it discriminates against the poor by focusing only on generally harmless activities that they need to engage in for survival. Furthermore, the legislation criminalizes homeless people simply for being homeless by targeting necessary survival strategies. Critics note that the Act was changed so that charities that engage in street level solicitations, such as firefighters and the Salvation Army, were excluded from prohibition.

In 2005 Toronto City Council voted to accept a proposal to ban homeless people from sleeping in Nathan Phillips Square. The amendment to By-law 1994-0784 specifically says, "no person can camp" (which includes sleeping in the Square during the day or night, whether or not a tent or temporary abode of any kind is used) "in the square." Incredibly, the Council went even further and decided to extend the ban to all City property.

This move to ban homeless people from sleeping in public spaces like Nathan Phillips Square is only part of a City Staff Report, "From the Street into Homes: A Strategy to Assist Homeless Persons to Find Permanent Housing." In discussing "ways to address street homelessness," the report also suggests "enhanced legal and legislative frameworks and more enforcement of current provincial laws and City by-laws." The report also "recommends that the Toronto Police Service be requested to participate in the work of the Street Outreach Steering Committee." Behind the report's velvety language of "outreach," one finds the iron fist of the Toronto Police.

This is no way to address homelessness in the City and is an open invitation for more attacks by cops on homeless people. It offers little more than an excuse to expand the already bloated Toronto Police budget that, at around $690 million, already gobbles up 22% of Toronto's property tax dollars.

In addition, ticketing and arrests under anti-poor law infractions such as the Safe Streets Act have already been stepped up. Young people have found themselves being held in jail for minor infractions and released on stringent bail conditions: not to possess cups and cleaning equipment, and prohibiting of access to parts of the city. Along with the massive ticketing, cops have used pepper spray to awaken youth sleeping on the streets.

The City has also revitalized a "park ambassador" program to move and harass homeless people in City parks. Along with their efforts to drive squeegee-ers out of the city, the cops have been busy chasing homeless people out of so-called "public parks." Poverty's okay, of course, just keep it out of sight.

Of course, a very real and vicious crackdown has been in effect for some time now. Police have routinely ticketed homeless people for trespassing, loitering, or littering. Likewise, some store owners make it a hobby to verbally or physically attack panhandlers or get the police to do it for them.

It is important to consider this recent and ongoing history of the City's prefer- ence for criminalizing homeless people rather than addressing root social and economic causes of homelessness, such as lack of affordable housing, availabil- ity of social services or access to jobs with a living wage. Council's proposed plans only serve to distort as criminal matters conditions that are fundamen- tally social and economic. People sleep at City Hall because the shelters are full and conditions in many of them are dreadful. People are forced to sleep outside because there's not enough truly affordable housing. By removing the homeless from the Square, the politicians hope to remove a major political embarrassment from under their noses.

Camping and (De)Criminalization in British Columbia

For those concerned about the criminalization of poor people in Canada, the October 14, 2008 judgement by B.C. Supreme Court Justice Carol Ross (*Vic- toria (City) v. Adams 2008 BCSC 1363*) confirmed their belief that the rights of poor and homeless people are being violated in B.C. The judgement regarded the constitutionality of Victoria city bylaws applied to prevent homeless peo- ple from sleeping overnight on public property or erecting temporary shelters to protect themselves against the elements.

The case dates from an initial 2005 challenge in which lawyers Boies Parker and Irene Faulkner argued that the application of Victoria's bylaws to prevent homeless people from sleeping overnight in parks, constituted a violation of rights under Sections 7 (security of the person) and 15 (equality before the law) of the Canadian Charter of Rights and Freedoms, because the city does not have sufficient shelter space to otherwise accommodate those in need. The initial case proceeded after a group of homeless people were arrested in

October 2005 for setting up a "tent city" in a Victoria park. Their eviction initiated the court challenge. There are approximately 1,500 people homeless in Victoria, according to the city's estimate, although such estimates are generally considered to be under-estimates given the difficulties of accessing many homeless people in street surveys or shelter counts. At the same time, the city has available only 331 shelter beds in the winter and 171 in the summer. Boies Parker argued that given that sort of broad imbalance, it is unconstitutional to prevent people from sleeping in city parks. Furthermore, if people need to sleep outside, they must be allowed to use a tarp or a tent as a form of temporary shelter against the elements. The lawyers argued that the ability to provide shelter for oneself is a fundamental right. In the absence of adequate alternatives, the city has no basis in which to deprive people of that right to shelter. Victoria's bylaw prevented the homeless from protecting themselves from the elements, which could lead to potentially fatal health risks.

In her 112-page Reasons for Judgment, Justice Ross found that sections of the Parks Regulation Bylaw and the Streets and Traffic Bylaw do "violate...the Canadian Charter of Rights and Freedoms in that they deprive homeless people of life, liberty, and security of the person in a manner not in accordance with the principles of fundamental justice." Justice Ross concluded that a sleeping bag or blanket does not provide enough protection from the elements for someone sleeping outside in B.C. The ruling also suggests that sleeping in a tent or similar structure is not a public safety issue, threatening the quality of life of others, but rather a matter of basic human dignity. According to Justice Ross, the insufficient capacity of Victoria's shelters leaves hundreds of homeless people with no choice but to sleep outside. Justice Ross wrote in her ruling: "I have concluded that the prohibition in the bylaws against the erection of temporary shelter in the form of tents, tarpaulins, cardboard boxes, or other structures exposes the homeless to a risk of significant health problems or even death."

Media in cities across Canada covered the story at a rather high pitch, suggesting the emergence of a moral panic much as occurred around squeegeeing prior to the passage of the Safe Streets Act. Some reports descended into the poor bashing identified by Swanson. Tom Fletcher of the *Surrey Leader* suggested the homeless of Victoria were "fake" and suggested that "the ruling leaves no way of sorting out the hobby-homeless. It denies the fact that when individuals start appropriating choice public property, they deprive the rest of us" (2008, 8). How could Fetcher identify the "hobby-homeless"? One of them was "mysteriously able to keep his long hair as neat as that of the earnest lawyers who enable his anarchist fantasies" (2008 8). Most reports spoke against the homeless, hardly any allowed them to speak. The voices privileged were those of civic and business officials.

Not surprisingly, those who had supported the bylaw and policies such as the Safe Streets Act and Downtown Ambassadors, were upset with the ruling. B.C. Housing Minister, Rich Coleman, called the ruling "ridiculous," while newspapers across the country warned of oncoming tent cities that would spring up in their cities. Acting chief of the Victoria Police Department Bill Naughton, suggested that the ruling would turn Victoria's parks into hubs for criminal activity, bringing illegal drugs and prostitution to the area.

The Victoria Chamber of Commerce harshly condemned the ruling. Its chief executive Bruce Carter repeated the assertion that parks are for families and children, rather than homeless people and counterpoised the rights of homeless people to the "public interest" as if homeless people's health and safety is something other than a public interest. In a statement, Carter asked: "How are our families and children, who pay taxes to maintain parks, supposed to get full enjoyment from parks when the homeless are given leave to camp in the playground" (Canadian Press 2008).

Victoria city council immediately announced that it will appeal the ruling. The city has itself been prone to moral panic over this case. In its submission to the court it asked: "What is to stop the overnight grad party or prostitute's tent" (Fletcher 2008, 8)? As if these are the same as camping as a last resort for shelter. The city continued: "Are all of our beaches to be open to addicts who may pass out in the sand where the syringes will fall" (Fletcher 2008, 8). As if all homeless people are addicts who leave syringes laying around. Poor bashing, indeed.

Police in Victoria have continued to evict people camping in city parks, up through the early months of 2011. Enforcement actions have been supported by an emergency bylaw city councillors passed as a way to restrict the court ruling. The new city policy permits temporary shelters only between the hours of 9 p.m. and 7 a.m., allowing police to take down any structures assembled outside of those hours. This has meant that police are now attending parks to roust homeless people who are camping after 7 a.m. Those who refuse to leave have their belongings confiscated and several have been arrested for obstruction. The new bylaw also prohibits the pitching of tents on sports fields, the children's playground, and environmentally sensitive parts of the park.

Despite the fact that the number of homeless people in Vancouver greatly outnumbers the amount of available shelter space, the City of Vancouver has asserted that the ruling does not apply to Vancouver since in the City's view the ruling only applies to the City of Victoria. The City argued that Vancouver has different legislation and bylaws, suggesting it would ignore the Supreme Court ruling. Vancouver mayor Gregor Robertson, a social democrat associated with the New Democratic Party, has publicly spoken out against tent cities and has refused to change the city's bylaw. At the same time, the housing ministry's own statistics show that there are more than 36,000 turnaways at shelters across Greater Vancouver over each recorded nine-month period.

Following the ruling, Pivot Legal Society launched a challenge in the B.C. Supreme Court that argues that Vancouver's anti-camping bylaws are also unconstitutional. That case will take some time yet before it reaches a judge. In response, groups of housing advocates attempted to sleep outside City Hall during a week-long fast. The city refused to allow them to set up tents in the rain. Anti-poverty advocates suggested that the decision could have positive impacts in supporting challenges to bylaws against sleeping outside that target the homeless across Canada, with some predicting the emergence of tent cities in other municipalities.

The B.C. Supreme Court decision must be contextualized within a broader, ongoing, political and social struggle over housing, citizenship, and rights in B.C. and across Canada. For some observers this will certainly be an area of ongoing contention, particularly as developments leading to and following up the 2010 Winter Olympics highlight tensions between urban development, land use, social policy, and the distribution of government resources and social funding in B.C.

On July 7, 2009 several homeless people, supported by the Anti-Poverty Committee, a direct action poor people's movement, established a tent city in an upscale neighbourhood at Vancouver's False Creek. The tent city was set up after condominium owners in the neighbourhood mobilized to compel City Council to close a temporary shelter in the neighbourhood, one of the areas that has seen much development both before and since the 2010 Winter Olympics and near the site of the troubled Athletes' Village project. That tent city survived almost one month. During the first week of February, 2011, organizers launched a follow up tent city to highlight the failure of governments, municipal and provincial, to come through with promised low income and below-market housing units that were pledged to be part of the Olympic legacy. Indeed, even promised units of the Athletes' Village were removed from social housing and sold on the market as an attempt to make up financial losses on the other units. Anti-poverty advocates suggest that these policies and housing decisions, including shelter closings in wealthier residential neighbourhoods, show the dual citizenship that is emerging in B.C. between privileged home owners and poor people who are denied even minimal shelter.

Conclusion

The recent anti-panhandling and anti-camping legislation, in various jurisdictions, show the way in which governments advocate for and implement legislation that does not necessarily reflect the concerns of the population more broadly. Critics note that there was no public outcry for such legislation prior to the moral panic instigated by local politicians. Furthermore there is little evidence to suggest that panhandling was a threat to public safety, or that the anti-panhandling laws have reduced street crimes or improved the safety of city streets. Critics suggest that, in fact, "Safe Streets" acts make life less safe for homeless people.

Numerous research projects, both prior to and since passage of the Safe Streets Act, have shown that homeless youth who were involved in squeegeeing in Ontario had less involvement in criminal activity and drug use than homeless youth who did not squeegee. Indeed, the government in Ontario had access to this research prior to the passage of the Act. Even more, the government could not present any legitimate or systematic evidence showing that squeegeeing and panhandling made cities in Ontario any less safe (O'Grady 2007).

The claim that parks are exclusively, or even primarily, for the use of children and families (of the housed), is in fact an ideological, and erroneous, political representation. Never mind that most of humanity has ranged over the land for most of human history. Never mind either that in many places the memory of the commons, prior to enclosure, still holds a powerful place in civic narratives, revived as environmental concerns have caused many to question the broad dangers of private ownership of the planet. More than that, there

Chapter 9: Homelessness, Criminalization, and the Right to Shelter

have been important moments in Canadian history when the poor and home-less have taken to camping in even relatively large number in parks and other "public" spaces. Certainly this was the case during the mass depressions of the 1910s and 1930s when economic troubles left many homeless. It was also a common occurrence in certain areas during the 1960s and 1970s, partly an expression of that desire for the commons. That the crisis of homelessness since the 1980s in Canada has led more to seek out this option as a means of sustenance or survival is not surprising. To ignore these facts is an act of erasure, an altering of Canadian history, particularly histories of poverty and inequality in Canada, for political ends.

CHAPTER 10

Sex Work, Criminalization, and the 2010 Olympics

The Vancouver-Whistler Olympic Winter Games took place on un-surrendered Native lands in British Columbia (B.C.), Canada, from February 12-27, 2010. For growing numbers of Indigenous people, anti-poverty activists, sex trade workers, homeless people, and low-income tenants, of Vancouver's Downtown Eastside (DTES) the Olympic Games, and growing practices of surveillance, harassment, arrest, and detention, represent a continued history of colonization and "social cleansing" of poor and marginalized communities. The development and social restructuring that were undertaken in the lead-up to the 2010 Games had severe negative impacts on communities that have suffered decades of conflict.

The present chapter specifically examines struggles over the sex trade, and the increased policing and punishment of sex trade workers as part of state policies of "social cleansing" in preparation for the Olympics. In all of this the views, perspectives, needs, and wishes of prostitutes are rarely taken into consideration. Thus, the chapter also examines attempts by sex trade workers themselves to establish alternative, self-determined, sex trade practices, such as a worker-controlled co-operatively run brothel, sex museum, and burlesque parlour as part of the grassroots response to Olympic-driven state initiatives. It also discusses debates and differences among sex trade workers over such responses.

Government policies and practices, which acted to criminalize, harass or remove sex trade workers from areas of the city slated for redevelopment in preparation for Olympic venues, tourist destinations, or residences during the

Games show aspects of the political economy of Olympic initiatives. Ongoing struggles over these policies and practices, and the activities of sex trade workers opposing their criminalization and seeking alternative working conditions, show also that such development is not unidirectional and uncontested. Rather possibilities open even for those whose presence is least desirable for the Olympic city and who lack socioeconomic resources.

Whose Streets? Social Cleansing, Sex Work, and 2010 ▬▬▬

Street prostitution in Vancouver is largely concentrated in downtown Vancouver, the so-called Downtown Eastside, and a nearby industrial area. The process by which the DTES evolved as the central area of the local sex trade began in the 1980s as prostitutes were forced out of neighbouring areas, notably Vancouver's West End, and the suburb of Burnaby. As a result of the rapid expansion in imported illegal drugs into the DTES during the 1990s, especially heroin and cocaine, and the proliferation of methamphetamine; a large number of prostitutes in the area are also drug addicted, and for many Vancouver residents, the connection between the sex and drug trades shapes perceptions of the former and has influenced calls for stronger policing in the area. At the same time this neighbourhood, the poorest in all of Canada, became a prime site of Olympic speculation, investment, and re-development as it is located near event venues as well as important transit hubs, including the downtown Skytrain rapid transit line and the Seabus linking Vancouver with North Vancouver and, from there, Whistler. Thus, this neighbourhood served as a focal point for some of the most intense struggles over social cleansing and Games development.

Visible street-based sex work in Vancouver, as in other Canadian cities, comes up against the property and profit concerns of legitimized business, commercial development and property speculators within specific neighbourhoods such as the DTES. These neighbourhoods undergo a conflictual process of transformation from local sites, residences and workplaces of the poor, to be made ready as sites for the enactment of global events such as the Olympics. To address their concerns, as business people, landlords, and investors vie for position within developing neighbourhoods, they, often successfully, bring pressure to bear against local politicians and police to act against sex trade workers (as has also been the case for homeless people). As Brooks (2002, 279) suggests: "Criminalizing the poor becomes a way of cleansing the city, making it a supposedly safe and attractive environment for affluent people." Often these affluent people are members of a global tourist class seeking anonymous pleasure in once distant locales.

Long serving British Columbia Premier Gordon Campbell, Premier during the Olympics, has suggested that sex work and homelessness are "Vancouver problems...not a West Vancouver [one of Canada's wealthiest municipalities] problem [not] a Port Moody problem, because they enforce their bylaws" (Laird 2007, 65). Former Premier Campbell has blamed prostitution, drug addiction, and a general unwillingness of people to abide by the laws for Vancouver's social problems.

In response to emerging issues of criminalization and marginalization, and the development of social policies and policing practices that target sex trade workers, homeless people, and street involved youth as part of the preparations for the 2010 Games, anti-Olympic organizers in Vancouver described what they view as a process of social cleansing that endangers women's lives. In the words of one opposition group: "Social cleansing has a deadly impact on any targeted community, and women are at even higher risk. Women who are homeless and trying to survive are pushed into even more dangerous situations, face prospects of having to stay in abusive relationships to maintain housing and are subject to endless harassment and violence on the street and in the shelter system" (Why We Resist 2007).

Part of the social regulation of sex trade workers includes the state's cuts to public health programs, income support, affordable housing programs, and childcare. In place of these social necessities, public money is directed toward policing, courts, and prison cells as well as privileges for elites, such as tax cuts, grants and spending on spectacles such as the Olympics.

In addition, the Olympics spurred a loss of already scarce affordable housing which has contributed to conditions of precarity. Since winning the 2010 Winter Games in 2003, Vancouver has lost more than 850 units of low-income housing, while during the same period homelessness has increased from 1,000 to more than 2,500 people. It was estimated that by 2010, the number of homeless would be as high as 6,000 and the number has grown since. Much of this increase has come from the large-scale closure of social housing and low-income hotels in Vancouver's Downtown Eastside, an area that is already the poorest neighbourhood in Canada. Closures have already been driven by the Olympics as developers seek to create more high-end, and high profit, spaces for tourists and corporate investors before and after the games. In Vancouver, anticipation of the 2010 Olympics led to rent increases and the transformation of low-income housing into upscale condos. According to the report "Fair Play for Housing Rights" by the Centre on Housing Rights and Evictions, Olympic Games have caused the displacement of over two million people since the 1980s (Centre on Housing Rights and Evictions 2007). In Seoul 1988, approximately 750,000 poor were displaced, while in Atlanta in 1996, more than 30,000 people were displaced. It is estimated that for Beijing in 2008, approximately 1.5 million have been displaced (Centre on Housing Rights and Evictions 2007).

As global capitalism develops, more and more poor and marginalized people are criminalized and punished (Bauman 1998). According to anti-poverty activist John Clarke of the Ontario Coalition Against Poverty (OCAP): "Acts of survival like petty drug dealing and prostitution are focused on but the real agenda is the 'social cleansing' of the [poor]" (quoted in Brooks 2002, 279). Examples of this agenda became regular features of social development in Vancouver as part of 2010 Olympic preparations. In the lead-up to the Games, this typically took the form of new by-laws and polices, such as Project Civil City, that arm police, business owners, and private security companies with a variety of means to harass street prostitutes and remove them from specific neighbourhoods. There was also an ongoing deployment of repressive policing practices, including "sweeps" of street involved people and the use of boundary conditions to prohibit prostitutes from even entering certain neighbourhoods near planned Olympic venues. These policies are not about public safety but about investment, redevelopment, and tourist dollars.

As Fedec (2002: 254), an RCMP officer, notes, current legislation and policing practices that deal with the sex trade in Canada are guided by assumptions that sex work is deviant and that those who engage in prostitution are morally impaired, whether through birth, socialization, or socioeconomic conditions. In labeling the women working in the sex trade as "criminal," society sidesteps the obligation to deal with underlying social inequalities that encourage such conditions (Brooks 2002, 279). Instead of addressing the roots of growing homelessness, poverty, and numbers of marginalized individuals, the criminal justice system is deployed to contain or erase, to "cleanse" cities of human manifestations of the problems of global capitalism. Ironically, perhaps, the pressures to hide these manifestations become most intense during festivals of global capital such as the Olympics, international film festivals, and the Football World Cup. These events serve to exacerbate conditions of suffering, exclusion, and desperation for the poorest and most marginalized of local populations in host cities (Center On Housing Rights and Evictions 2007).

Even greater irony, given the criminalization of sex trade workers in the lead-up to the 2010 Winter Games, was the expectation, noted by police at all levels, that demand for prostitutes would, in fact, grow dramatically during the Games. Spectacular events such as the Olympics, which draw hundreds of thousands of male tourists with disposable income and the cover of anonymity contribute to large increases in prostitution and trafficking of women. One social impact that is a regular feature of the Olympic Games is the increase in the trafficking of women and prostitution. In Seoul 1988, there was increased prostitution for the Games. In the Athens Games of 2004, 40,000 prostitutes were brought in from Asian countries and elsewhere. This trafficking is carried out by violent networks that subject women to abuse, torture, and identity theft. Such was expected in Vancouver for the 2010 Olympics according to the Vancouver Police Department (VPD). Yet, despite this, little attention has been given to conditions that would make sex work safer for sex workers under these conditions. Little focus has been placed on, even known, trafficking networks or on what I call "demand-side" policing, that might shift attention toward potential johns in the lead-up to the Games.

As opponents of 2010 noted, this is particularly troubling given the recent history of violence, including the abductions and murders of sex trade workers in Vancouver over the last decade. More than 68 women are missing and/or have been murdered in Vancouver alone. Many were Native, and many were reportedly involved in the sex trade. A Joint Taskforce of the Royal Canadian Mounted Police and the Vancouver Police Department investigating the disappearances reports that at least sixteen of the missing women are Indigenous, a number that greatly exceeds the proportion of women living in Vancouver. Unfortunately police had refused to devote resources to investigate the disappearances, denying that there was any pattern or particular danger despite the backgrounds of the women and their connections with the sex trade.

In northern B.C., more than 30 young women, mostly Native, are missing and/or murdered along Highway 16, a route that has been dubbed "the highway of tears." Unfortunately, despite disappearances of Indigenous women over a decade, it was only in 2002, following the disappearance of a non-Indigenous woman, that the media and police focused any attention on the disappearances and killings. While government practices, legislation and policing fail to address these realities, street prostitution remains among the most dangerous jobs in Canada (Lowman 2000).

Shifting Ground: Sex Trade Legislation in Canada ▰▰▰▰▰▰

Perspectives, legal and social, on prostitution in Canada have varied widely over time and place. Often at the centre of moral panics, prostitution has been targeted as a threat to public health as well as signaling the decline of moral order in the country. For others, particularly business owners, prostitution has been viewed as a nuisance activity serving to drive away customers from commercial areas. For land developers and landowners, prostitution poses a threat to property values and rental profits. More recently, as prostitution has become more prevalent in suburban areas outside of the city core, residents and homeowners associations have spoken against prostitution as a threat to children and property values alike (Brock 1998; Lowman 2000).

Many Canadian citizens are unaware that prostitution is not illegal in Canada. Instead, laws have focused on peripheral issues related to prostitution, such as publicly communicating with another person to sell, or less frequently, to buy sexual services or operating a bawdy house. It remains a controversial issue, however, one that has received a great deal of attention by various levels of government, police, and local business associations. Street prostitution in particular has been the target of legislation and policing, a fact that is reflected in laws against public communication for purposes of selling sex. Despite the failure to formally declare prostitution an illegal activity, legislative responses and popular discourses alike have generally treated street prostitution as criminal activity and prostitutes as criminals engaged in illegal and immoral behaviour (Melrose 2003; Fedec 2002; Lowman 2000; Brock 1998).

At various times in Canadian history, state and social approaches to prostitution have shifted, reflecting a certain ambiguity over whether or not prostitution is a victimless crime, a voluntary exchange, a social harm, or an outright crime. The changing legal approaches to prostitution show the ambivalence of state and civil society actors toward prostitution. Laws governing the sex trade have rather consistently targeted the most visible expressions of adult prostitution while never quite formally prohibiting the exchange of sex for money. Until the early 1970s, prostitution was treated as a "status" offence, akin to vagrancy (Duchesne 1997). Anyone working in a public place who could not provide an acceptable reason for being there, could be arrested and charged. The soliciting law introduced in 1972 emphasized specific behaviours by prohibiting anyone from soliciting another in a public place for prostitution. This legislation proved difficult for authorities to enforce, however, since "public place" was not clearly defined (were vehicles included for example), many sexual services were not covered and it did not apply to clients as well as sex workers (Duchesne 1997). In addition, solicitation had to meet the requirement of being "pressing and persistent," which was a matter of perspective.

In light of the dissatisfaction of police and courts with the legislative tools available to criminalize prostitution, the newly elected Conservative government of Prime Minister Brian Mulroney undertook a series of consultations to assess the adequacy of existing laws on prostitution. As an outcome of these consultations, in December 1985, the "communicating" law replaced the soliciting law (Duchesne 1997). It is this law that governs prostitution to this day. The central concern of the communicating law has been to target street prostitution, making it less visible. While the law does not make the sale of sexual services illegal, it does criminalize public communication for purposes of selling or buying sexual services.

The consultations that gave rise to the communication law were marked by an outward concern, driven by business associations and developers, about the economic costs of a visible sex trade presence. Since the introduction of the communicating law, the focus of arrests has been on street prostitutes. Indeed, within a decade of the communicating law's introduction, the overwhelming majority of prostitution arrests involved street communication (92%), compared to procuring (5%) and bawdy house incidents (3%) (Duchesne 1997). That contrasts rather dramatically with the numbers from the final year under the soliciting law, in which most incidents involved bawdy houses (58%) rather than soliciting (22%) (Duchesne 1997).

As Fedec (2002, 253) notes, the various laws in Canadian history have been consistent in targeting the sellers of sex for violating moral and social codes of conduct, but have rarely targeted the purchasers of sexual services. Sexually exploited women and children continue to be indicted as offenders by local communities and the law, even where they are victims of abuse by male purchasers (Fedec 2002, 254). Police practices make social relations of exploitation and predation worse. Buyers of sexual services, typically more privileged and financially advantaged, are rarely targets of the legal system in Canada.

Issues of power and control are not only expressed in sex trade interactions, but in police charging practices as well. According to Fedec (2002) more than 90% of charges are placed against the sex trade worker, while fewer than 10% of charges are against a male customer, even after implementation of a 1983 amendment that extended liability to customers. Such rates persisted even with the shift toward communicating for sexual services, clearly a dialogic event involving at least two people. Such legal practices shift emphasis of responsibility away from the more privileged customers who create the demand for the sex trade. Policing discrepancies also relate to detection and conviction rates. Because enforcement officials need to maintain arrest rates, street prostitutes provide the most appealing targets because they rarely beat charges in court.

Despite the fact that prostitution itself remains legal, the communicating law established no clear guidelines on where it can take place. On the whole, an evaluation by the Department of Justice in 1989 declared the legislation ineffective in reducing street prostitution (Duchesne 1997). At the same time, the ambiguity and lack of clarity in the law has given local law enforcement agencies a broad scope of application of the law based on their own needs and interpretations. Such leeway was routinely exercised by police in the lead-up to the Olympics.

Uncivil City: 2010 and the Criminalization of Sex Work in Vancouver

Prostitutes, unlike clients, are perceived to be part of a criminal underclass or subculture, associated with thefts and drugs, and treated accordingly. The arrests of prostitutes and their removal from areas near Olympic venues can be portrayed, as police have attempted to do, as part of a broader security strategy focused on these other offences. Such has been the case particularly in light of the concerns over gang violence, and the association of gangs with the drug trade in Vancouver.

This ongoing practice of what I prefer to call supply-side policing is reinforced in pre-Olympic policing policies and practices that exclusively focus on street sweeps of prostitutes and the use of boundary conditions that prohibit sex trade workers even from being present in the planned Olympic zones near venue sites. Despite the fact that government cuts to social services, and the transfer of public funds toward Olympic spending, along with gentrification and the loss of affordable housing, will only serve to increase the numbers of people living or working on the streets, local governments continued to develop policies focusing on "cleaning up" Vancouver in time for the Games. Municipal governments in Vancouver have made it clear throughout the period leading up to the Olympics that they want to hide visible manifestations of poverty, drug use, and the sex trade in the DTES. This has resulted in the development and implementation of a number of policies and practices targeting street-involved people, including sex trade workers and homeless people in the city core.

Policies such as the Safe Streets Act have given police and local businesses a legislative tool to punish a range of survival strategies of street-involved people, including squeegeeing, panhandling, and solicitation in roadways. Perhaps the most troubling policy initiative has been the Civil City Act, which targets a range of street activities and extends policing beyond public forces, providing business associations broad leeway to intervene. The program includes hundreds of thousands of dollars for increased private security, in addition to regular city police budgets and the approximately one billion dollars being directed toward Olympic security. The Civil City initiative was explicitly designed to target street prostitutes, panhandlers, and open drug users in specific areas such as the DTES. Such policies do nothing to address underlying issues of poverty, precarious housing, drug abuse, or unemployment. They are effective at removing people from the streets and getting them into custody.

In addition, following the awarding of the Olympics to Vancouver, the city initiated a "street ambassadors" program in which public money was directed to business improvement associations to hire private security firms to patrol downtown streets and clear areas of street prostitutes and homeless people. The so-called Downtown Ambassadors have been given free reign to intimidate and harass people deemed to be "undesirables." The behaviors of "street ambassadors" have been highly dubious, regularly violating people's civil rights. Indeed, the situation has deteriorated to such a degree that the Pivot Legal Society, an anti-poverty law group, has called on the city to end the "street ambassador" program, releasing a report that documented ongoing abuse by "ambassadors" toward street involved people in several neighbourhoods (Lupick, 2008b). Pivot Legal Society, the Vancouver Area Network of Drug Users (VANDU) and the United Native Nations have filed a Human Rights complaint against the Downtown Vancouver Business Improvement

Association (DVBIA) and Geoff Plant, the Civil City Commissioner. The complaint was filed on behalf of Vancouver's street population and alleges systemic discrimination by the Downtown Ambassadors program, which is run by Genesis Security and the DVBIA under the guidance of Geoff Plant. The complaint identifies a number of behaviors it calls discriminatory, including compelling people who are sitting or sleeping on the street to move along, regardless of location or circumstances; telling people to stop searching for recyclables in garbage cans; identifying particular individuals as undesirable and telling them that they are not allowed within a particular geographic area, so-called "no go areas"; and following or staring at and taking notes and photographs of individuals identified as undesirable (Lupick 2008a).

Policies such as Civil City and the Safe Streets Act provide other tools for targeting younger sex trade workers. Typically, younger sex trade workers have not been charged with communicating. Rather, they have been criminalized for other offences, such as vandalism, theft or drug possession (Fedec, 2002). More recently, policies such as Civil City and Safe Streets allow police to criminalize street involved youth for jaywalking, squeegeeing, panhandling, or simply loitering. Police criminalize street youth as means to facilitate intervention by social services, declaring homeless or street involved youth under the age of 16 to be wards of the state. Intervention almost invariably has meant placing youth in the care of foster or group homes or with child protection agencies or returning them to the very home situations from which they had escaped (Fedec 2002, 261). It has not involved independent, supportive living.

In addition, other Olympic inspired by-laws target the basic everyday living activities of street prostitutes and homeless people. Newly installed benches make it impossible for people to stretch out and many bus shelters have removed benches altogether. New garbage canisters on streets make it more difficult for people to gather recyclables. In addition, a newly introduced by-law removes large garbage bins from the DTES.

These measures have been established within an overall plan to remove downtown residents from the area. In addition to jail, some have been removed to mental institutions and others to "detox" centres on former military bases. Another measure has removed people from the province entirely through a "fly-back" program in which the B.C. Government pays the costs to return persons wanted on warrants in other provinces.

Vancouver police publicly stated, and recently confirmed, that street prostitutes, as well as homeless people, would be removed from Olympic zones across Vancouver throughout the period of the Olympics (Dembicki 2009). This has involved the physical removal of people within areas near Olympic venues. These areas cover several blocks in radius from the site and prevented street-involved people from accessing some of their everyday necessities, such as community centres, which are only located in specific areas such as the DTES.

In the lead-up to the Games, particularly in 2008 and 2009, police practiced extensive ticketing against street workers. Tickets were leveled for minor activities such as jaywalking, spitting, and abusive language. The Pivot Legal Society, reported large increases in the numbers of people approaching them about tickets for minor infractions (Chan 2009; Hill 2009). The Vancouver Police Department (VPD) has itself confirmed in a year-end performance report that officers issued 467 tickets for violations of the Safe Streets Act in 2008. That compared with 202 tickets in 2007. Police officers also handed out 133 tickets for violations of the Trespass Act, up from 95 in 2007. The number of tickets issued for city-bylaw infractions, including tickets for vending, panhandling, and loitering, ballooned to 439 tickets in 2008 compared with 247 tickets in 2007. The VPD's draft business plan for 2009 called for a further increase in ticketing by at least 20% as well as increases to the number of officers on Beat Enforcement Teams. The plan also included a target of "a minimum of 4 street checks per BET member per block" (Chan 2009; Hill 2009). Tickets have clearly been used as a means to drive people from the DTES. Even more, people receiving tickets have received boundary conditions prohibiting them from being in the DTES, an obvious attempt to sweep them out of the area.

The approach taken by city and provincial governments in preparation for the 2010 Winter Olympics was almost exclusively to utilize the services of law enforcement agencies to enforce by-laws and punitive policies such as Civil City. These practices were directed at displacing the marginalized and poor and fail to address issues of poverty, housing, unemployment, and cuts to social spending and public assistance programs that have accompanied the Olympics as public spending was shifted largely toward Olympic projects. This displacement only affects the visibility and location of street involved residents of Vancouver. Such criminalization practices do not meet any real social need, particularly those of residents of the DTES. Social policy might be directed toward decreasing child exploitation, abuse of women, drug addiction and health issues, including the HIV-AIDS epidemic in the DTES, but in the context of Olympic hegemony such policy questions have been pushed to the margins, barely audible in public discourse. Reducing social assistance and support programs have only made matters worse. Enforcement of discriminatory laws against street involved residents of the DTES, a true legacy of the 2010 Games, suggests a shift in Canadian citizenship in which rights are reserved for global elites of the tourist classes at the expense of poor residents.

Colonialism by Other Means?

In Canada, the primary victims of "street trade women abuse" come from marginalized communities (Fedec 2002, 254). In their report on discrimination and violence against Indigenous women in Canada, Amnesty International noted: "The social and economic marginalization of Indigenous women, along with a history of government policies that have torn apart Indigenous families and communities, have pushed a disproportionate number of Indigenous women into dangerous situations that include extreme poverty, homelessness, and prostitution." The legacy of colonialism is key to the over-representation of Natives in the sex trade in Canada, having pushed Native children and youth into street life and crimes of economic necessity (Royal Commission on Aboriginal Peoples 1997; Gilchrist and Winchester 1997; Fedec 2002). In Vancouver, indigenous children and youth of both sexes are regularly present on the streets providing sex, primarily to middle-class, employed, white married men (Fedec 2002, 257).

The long history of racial and class oppression has had numerous negative impacts on indigenous communities, including suicides, physical and sexual abuse, lower levels of educational attainment, limited access to financially sustainable jobs, cultural alienation, over-criminalization and presence in the criminal justice system, particularly for non-violent crimes and crimes of economic necessity (Fedec 2002). The legacy of colonial dispossession and cultural erasure has also left Indigenous women living in urban centres in Canada vulnerable to heightened levels of violence. Generations of Indigenous women and girls have been dispossessed and displaced by government policies and corporate activities.

Many now face desperate circumstances in Canadian towns and cities, a situation compounded by sexist stereotypes and racist attitudes toward Indigenous women and girls and general indifference to their welfare and safety. The result has been far too many Indigenous women and girls placed in harm's way, denied adequate protection from law, and marginalized in a way that allows some men to get away with carrying out violent crimes against them (Amnesty International 2004).

Almost 60% of Indigenous people in British Columbia currently live off reserve in urban areas. One quarter of Indigenous families live in inadequate housing. One quarter of households is headed by a single mother. As Bramham (2008) notes: "Mothers and grandmothers often carry the heaviest burden. They are more likely to live in poverty and experience violence than any other men or women in Canada."

These specific conditions, however, must be contextualized and understood as specific moments in an extensive, and ongoing, history of dislocation, displacement, cultural erasure and genocide. Throughout Canadian history, "the land and resource base essential to the viability of Indigenous economies and ways of living has been dramatically eroded by the failure of governments to consistently recognize and uphold Indigenous title" (Amnesty International, 2004). For contemporary Indigenous activists, the 2010 Olympics represent a continuation of those historical practices by which the land and resource bases of Indigenous communities are stripped further from those communities and the cultures that rely upon them are rendered even more precarious. This is displacement and dislocation by other names: tourism and economic development.

Emerging Resistance

Sex trade workers mobilized as part of the opposition to the Olympics in Vancouver's poorest neighbourhood, organizing ongoing mass demonstrations protesting police sweeps and the ticketing of sex trade workers. As part of a grassroots response to Olympic-driven state initiatives punishing sex trade workers, sex trade workers have also attempted to establish alternative, self-determined, sex trade practices, such as a worker-controlled co-operatively run brothel, sex museum and burlesque parlour.

Among the groups that have been most active in opposing the criminalization of poor and marginalized communities has been the Downtown Eastside Women's Centre. In addition to mobilizing large numbers to confront police and their ticketing policies, they have actively worked to fight tickets in the courts. Organizer Angela Sterritt, an artist and writer from the Gitxsan Nation of Northwest British Columbia, who works as a support worker in the Downtown Eastside Women's Centre and helped found the Native 2010 Resistance, undertook a cross-country speaking tour to raise awareness about the harms being done in preparation for the Olympics.

The criminalization of sex work in the lead-up to the 2010 Winter Games not only focused on sex workers on the streets but also on sex workers organizing against the 2010 Games and the practices of criminalization against prostitutes, homeless, and poor people. Repression involved attacks on anti-Olympic groups and individuals, including arrests of protesters, raids of offices, surveillance, media smear campaigns, cuts to funding programs, and so on; all in an effort to undermine anti-2010 resistance. This repression was early deployed against sex workers, women's rights groups, anti-poverty and housing groups, environmentalists, and Natives, in Vancouver.

The criminalization of dissent was part of the preparation for the massive security operations instituted for the Games. As many as 13,000 police and military personnel were available to patrol the Games and demonstrations. In addition, CCTV video surveillance cameras were installed throughout the downtown and crowd control fencing was used to construct special security zones. The overall cost of policing the Games, posted at $75 million in the initial proposal to the International Olympic Committee (IOC), eventually came to be pegged at at least $1 billion in real costs. All of that was covered by public funds, money that is taken from federal, provincial, and municipal budgets for social services, health care, and education.

From Criminalization to Celebration: Experiential Women and the Cooperative Brothel

In response to the dangers facing sex workers in Vancouver and the challenges of dealing with stepped up policing in advance of the 2010 games, a group of Vancouver sex workers came together to organize the first cooperatively run brothel in Canada. The co-op brothel was intended as a first step in attempting to provide women a safe place to work, with health and safety provisions, and free from the exploitation of pimps. The co-op planning group, which developed out of a pre-existing Vancouver-based sex workers' alliance, the British Columbia Coalition of Experiential Women, incorporated and quickly began laying the groundwork to establish the co-op brothel. Part of that work has included the difficult tasks of outreach and communication to develop agreeable relations with trade unions, local businesses, and police.

For the experiential women planning the co-op brothel, their vision calls forth a space that would usher in a "golden age of sex work," with bawdy houses operating freely under the direction of sex workers themselves (Leung 2007; Lee 2007; Joyce 2008). Not simply interested in opening a brothel, the group has a broad and vibrant vision of creating a space that would form the centre of a celebration of sex and sex work. Their overall plan includes a museum and gallery to showcase the artwork and history of showgirls and prostitutes. It would also include a dinner club with burlesque performances within the same complex as the brothel (Leung 2007; Lee 2007; Joyce 2008).

Organizers have proposed a members-run system in which any sex worker could join for a nominal fee and be able to rent clean rooms at low cost. Expenses would be shared but members would have the autonomy to determine their own fees and retain all of their profits. The brothel planners have held early talks with labour organizers to discuss health and safety practices and the co-op members would enforce labour standards.

According to organizer Susan Davis, the sex workers' group aimed to have the co-op brothel and burlesque hall fully operating in time for the arrival of tourists for the 2010 Games. Because the Olympic organizing committee's mandate promised support for local economic development, brothel backers have suggested that the cooperative should be included as an equal with other legitimized projects. Providing a viable, and demanded, business while offering a safer space for sex trade workers would seem to meet local economic and social development needs of the DTES more so certainly than the conversion of low rent hostels to high end condos. Even more it reflects the sociocultural history of the area, and the concerns of some longtime residents and workers, more than the gentrifying practices that the various levels of government have favoured.

In order to address the legal restrictions on sex work in Canada, and the fact that most activities associated with it are criminalized, including soliciting sexual services in public places; operating a bawdy house and living off the avails of prostitution, the group was faced with having to appeal to the federal government for an exemption (Joyce, 2008). In this there is some precedence. The government has already provided a temporary exemption to allow the operation of a supervised injection site in the city on a provisional "test-case" basis. In the words of brothel planner Susan Davis: "We can't do anything that would put police in a position to arrest us. So, what we're saying is, 'This is such a little place. Let us try and demonstrate to you what we think will happen, which is it will greatly diminish the complaints from the neighbour-hood and will greatly increase the safety of the sex workers of the Downtown Eastside'" (quoted in Leung 2007).

Faced with the enormous range of efforts involved in preparing the city to host the 2010 Winter Olympics, Vancouver authorities initially expressed some willingness to at least consider the proposal, partly as a means to free up resources for other undertakings. According to Vancouver police spokes-person Howard Chow: "We would be willing to explore anything that...would be helping the situation of sex trade workers, and make it safer for them and make it better for the community" (quoted in Leung 2007). Chow noted one reservation: "It has to be something that is lawful" (quoted in Leung 2007).

The strongest early opposition to the co-op brothel plan came, not from police or local politicians, but from escort agency operators fearful of the prospects of facing a prominent and well organized competition. Interestingly, strong opposition also came from some former sex workers and progressive women's organizations. Members of the Vancouver Rape Relief and Women's Shelter publicly expressed their objections to the idea of the co-op brothel. In their view, prostitution is a means of perpetuating violence against women regard-less of where it is practiced or under what conditions. They argue that given a choice, an overwhelming majority of prostitutes would leave the sex trade. As spokesperson Daisy Kler has stated in response to the proposed brothel plans: "The idea that there are women who, given an autonomous decision, given all other options, would stay is a fantasy" (quoted in Leung 2007). Fur-thermore, from their perspective, a co-op would not protect Vancouver's most vulnerable women, as street prostitutes might not have the money to join. In any event, the brothel is, for Kler, only a place in which men can continue to exploit women: "We don't think men should be entitled to buy and sell

Chapter 10: Sex Work, Criminalization, and the 2010 Olympics

women to satiate themselves" (quoted in Leung 2007). The response that they advocate alternatively is one that relies on police targeting pimps and johns.

Brothel planners agree that those women who wish to leave the sex trade should be supported in doing so. At the same time they assert their right to engage in sex work and seek to improve the conditions in which their work is undertaken and to develop some autonomy and control over those conditions. As Susan Davis suggests, in response to critics like Kler: "This is hard for feminists to swallow. Having your own destiny is really appealing to everyone. There's a lot of people with no lived experience trying to impose what they think is right on us" (quoted in Leung 2007).

The proposed brothel received support from some frontline workers in the area who see it as one way to provide an alternative "real world" option for sex workers to begin more adequately addressing the violence of street work in the Downtown Eastside. Kerry Porth and Sheri Kiselbach, coordinators of the Prostitution Alternatives Counselling and Education Society, note that despite the high profile and outrage over the Pickton trial, little has been done to improve the safety of sex workers in Vancouver. Indeed, on the contrary, the increased policing, harassment and criminalization of sex workers as part of the Olympic redevelopments in the DTES have only made conditions less safe for sex workers who feel compelled to take the trade into hidden corners and alleyways, and who are more fearful about approaching police or local authorities about their concerns. The sex trade has been pushed further underground, forcing women to work in isolation in dangerous conditions (Lowman 2000; Fedec 2002; Melrose 2003; Leung 2007).

Street prostitutes continue to be victimized by violent clients in Vancouver. While opponents of the cooperative brothel disagree, much research (Fedec, 2002; Melrose, 2003) suggests that the incidence of violence is greatly reduced, though certainly not eliminated, when sex workers move from the streets to indoor venues such as massage parlors or escort services. "Every time you go out there, you don't know what's going to happen," Porth said. "You don't know if it's your last night out there and that's a ridiculous amount of stress for any individual to live with."

Initially, politicians and local businesses expressed some support for the plan. However, opposition began to grow as local businesses, and especially land developers in the Downtown Eastside became queasy about the prospects of having a burlesque hall and brothel in their neighbourhood. In addition, the federal Conservative government, which owes much of its grassroots support to social conservatives who abhor open and frank displays or discussions of sexuality and which has already tried to shut down the safe injection site, has made clear its unwillingness to grant any exemption for a brothel. The first vote on the brothel saw the plan defeated. The experiential women remain undeterred however, and it is anticipated a reworked plan will be re-introduced.

The often hostile debate over the brothel proposal shows the divergent views on prostitution even within sex worker communities and progressive women's organizations. For the Coalition of Experiential Women, sex *work* is simply that, a form of wage labour like any other in which labourers sell their bodies (labour power in Marxist terms) for pay. This is a materialist approach that holds that within a capitalist society, most people are compelled to sell themselves to someone else and, short of ending the wage relation, the real questions are over the conditions in which one works and the degrees of autonomy and workplace control one experiences. Arguments that such work objectifies women and reduces them to bodily characteristics is met with the response that similar reductions are suffered by construction workers, farm labourers, or anyone involved in forms of manual labour. This echoes socialist feminist analyses or intersections of exploitation and oppression.

On the other hand some sex worker critics and shelter workers provide a moral response in opposing the co-op brothel. They suggest that sex work is inherently oppressive and degrading of women. This is akin to radical feminist perspectives that view sex work as expressive of patriarchal relations more broadly, regardless of context or the condition in which services are provided. In this view, no sex work is safe or healthy sex work.

This debate has brought to the forefront different approaches to policing practices and criminalization of sex trade workers in Vancouver. Notably sex workers who oppose the brothel favour the criminalization of sex work, if not of sex workers. They prefer to work with police to develop practices that focus on johns, pimps, and traffickers rather than the sweeps, harassment, and arrests of sex trade workers. Some Experiential Women seek legalization to bring sex work within a legal framework of labour law and workplace rights and obligations. This would see health and safety regulations and labour codes apply to the sex trade industry on the whole. Still other Experiential Women prefer a decriminalization approach that seeks not legalization and regulation but asks police and legislators to allow sex workers to practice their trade unimpeded and to regulate themselves.

For sex trade workers, regardless of the debate on the rights and wrongs of the sex trade, a proactive and positive approach to sex workers' safety, one initiated and driven by sex workers is desperately needed (Leung 2007; Joyce 2008). As Susan Davis suggests: "We can continue the debate about morality. I don't think that should stop...but we can't deny it exists. I mean how moral is it to let people die" (quoted in Leung 2007)? For supporters of the brothel plan, the development of a co-op brothel may also help to spare more sex trade workers from criminalization. Lower status prostitutes are typically the ones targeted by police and other law enforcement officials. Street prostitutes rather than higher priced escorts and massage parlour workers are most often criminalized, and typically subjected to harsher punishments.

Conclusion

Opponents of the 2010 Olympics expressed concerns that the Games would only increase this violence against women. This is especially likely given that, as part of economic restructuring to fund the Olympics, the provincial government has cut funding for social programs, social housing, and healthcare programs that poor and homeless women and women working in the sex trade rely on.

Government expenditures on the Games, including the expected billion dollars spent on policing, total approximately 6 billion dollars which will be paid for through public debt. That is money that could have been spent on social services, housing, education, unemployment insurance, drug treatment, healthcare, and so on.

For the urban poor of Vancouver, which includes many Natives, 2010 has already meant hundreds evicted from low-income housing, more homelessness, criminalization, and increased police repression against sex trade workers. Aggressive policing in the Downtown Eastside has also involved immigration officers targeting immigrants. Indigenous women have been targeted by the state for punishment. In some cases, Indigenous women have received harsher penalties than other, non-Native, protesters.

Sex workers played central roles in the movements emerging to contest the character of the 2010 Winter Olympics, both at the grassroots level and as national and international spokespeople. This movement provides a compelling model for the development of a global movement. It highlights important connections between economic liberalism, displacement of local communities and violence, including state violence, particularly against women. It also shows some of the organizing work that can be done to address these interconnected issues in a manner that brings together people of diverse backgrounds. Because of the many diverse social issues and communities 2010 negatively impacts, there is much potential for a strong post-Olympics opposition movement to develop. It might also provide a catalyst from which new social movements and organizations working for sex workers' rights can emerge.

CHAPTER 11

Capital Offenses: Elite Crime and Deviance

P erpetrators of corporate deviance, who profit from unsafe working conditions for their employees, the release of dangerous toxins into the air and water, the sale of faulty products and fraudulent business practices among other acts; present ongoing economic, social, and physical threats. Yet those responsible for such activities rarely appear in the media or court records. They receive far less attention than deviant youth whose actions may be much less harmful. The crimes of major corporations, where they are given attention are typically dealt with through less visible and less punitive civil procedures rather than criminal trials. While school crime and deviance undertaken by working class youth become the subjects of moral panics and policing, and have relatively large amounts of social resources directed toward stopping the offending behavior; corporate crimes receive relatively little media focus, public outcry or legislative response. Critical theorists question why it is that the waters are being drugged with harmful chemicals yet attention is directed toward arresting youth for minor drug offences, including strictly personal use.

Notions of crime are constructed in relation to who holds power. Poor people's lives are more closely and more frequently regulated. It is the poor, rather than elites who are viewed as the "dangerous classes" in society. The poor are blamed for their social conditions rather than economic and political structures and relationships.

Significantly, and unfortunately, criminology has too often reinforced the emphasis on non-elites and the shifting of focus away from social, political, and economic structures. Theories that accept state definitions of crime and deviance, and place blame on the individual, separated from social contexts, fail to address structures of power, exploitation, and inequality in society that shape crime and punishment. Constructing crime as predominantly "street crime" supports status quo power relations and shifts attention away from the massive crime and harms inflicted on society by elites, while blowing out of proportion the often minor harms caused by non-elite activities.

Dangerous Classes: Real and Perceived

All of this is part of the ongoing attempts by states and capital to present the working classes and poor people as primary threats to social order and peace. Certainly elites have been, and continue to be effective in this. It has always been members of the working classes who have been the targets of criminalization. The legal and correctional systems of liberal democracies are based on this. The overwhelming majority of people processed through the criminal justice systems in countries like Canada have been, historically and at present, working class and poor people. Almost all involve petty property crimes and low level street crimes. The working classes, especially the poorest, are presented as the "dangerous class." Their lives are more regulated, and in neo-liberal regimes poverty is re-moralized as personal failing rather than economic structure.

Crime problems are constructed as being "street crimes" (like vandalism and property damage during a protest). "Suite crime," the crimes of elites (such as those meeting behind the security fence), receives minimal attention and scorn. Yet suite crime is more injurious. While street crimes tend to have a low level, localized impact involving one or two people immediately involved (and often with no victim physically harmed since damage is to property), suite crime typically has profoundly injurious impacts on individuals (including workers who are hurt and killed), communities, and the environment. It is resonant damage and spreads over space and time, impacting many (as in a chemical spill that hurts the workers in a workplace, communities that have to be evacuated, and water and air that are contaminated) in a way that goes well beyond the impacts of street crime.

Even if one considers the most extreme instances, particularly involving death, the numbers are telling. In Canada, in 2005, there were 655 murders.

In 2007, 594 murders. These killings are the basis for much panic and anxiety and serve to justify policy expenditures, "get tough on crime" legislation and "law and order" media stories. Yet, if one looks at another cause of avoidable death in Canada, namely workplace deaths, the comparison is stark. In 2005, at least 1,097 people died simply trying to earn a living. In 2007, the number was more than 1,005. In 2003, the homicide rate was 1.7 per 100,000 in Canada but the rate of work-related deaths was 6.1 per 100,000. These numbers are actually undercounts since they only record deaths accepted within workplace compensation boards (and arbitrarily exclude dangerous occupations like farm labour). Imagine if murders were recorded so ideologically. Yet there is little public outcry, no legislative mobilization, and virtually no coverage.

Indeed, most of these deaths would fit the definition some give for crime: avoidable misconduct that causes unnecessary harm to individuals or society. When bosses cut corners on safety equipment and someone dies. When there is a speed up or lack of training or working shorthanded and someone is killed or maimed. When proper treatment facilities are not installed in order to keep costs down and profits up.

Occupational death is the third leading cause of death in Canada (more than motor vehicle accidents). Yet suite crime is not treated as crime, and politicians and bosses responsible are not held to account. These are crimes against the person, more devastating than the property crimes for which non-elites are typically punished. These harms will not even be called what they are or considered crimes. The people responsible will be treated as "community leaders" and feted during parties like the G8/G20. They are the real dangerous classes — those who willfully and carelessly damage individuals, communities, and nature in pursuit of property and profit. They, and their actions, are the real issue at hand, not the street level actions of those who would oppose them.

Safety standards in Canada and the U.S. are routinely ignored, violated, or simply insufficient to meet the tasks required for health and safety. Millions of Canadians and Americans experience shortened lives, pain, and illness because of the actions of corporations and governments. Government intervention is infrequent and minimal. Penalties are usually avoided and when applied are trivial. They are nowhere near the response and outlay of resources deployed to address minor property crimes.

When workers do come forward to claim compensation through public workplace insurance boards, it is often they who are treated as the guilty parties. Workers making claims are often subjected to stressful and difficult tests and procedures by unsympathetic government and corporation-appointed doctors who are concerned with maintaining corporate profitability. These cases can drag out for years, adding to physical and financial stresses for workers. Corporations have access to well paid and effective legal teams for representation while workers are left to fend for themselves without any representation of guidance. Often companies and compensation boards will spy on injured workers to see if they are engaging in even routine tasks like gardening or playing with children. Such activities will then be used against claimants. Often injuries are not recognized, as was the case for generations with repetitive strain injuries and carpel tunnel syndrome. Many women had to fight to have these injuries recognized before insurance boards and employers that claimed the injuries were caused by knitting or childcare. Thus, patriarchal views and sexism were added to class disadvantage.

Excusing Elite Deviance

If we define crime as avoidable misconduct that causes unnecessary harm or damage to society, then it is clear that much of the activities engaged by economic and political elites could and should be considered criminal. White collar and corporate crimes, such as selling unsafe products, unhealthy workplaces, pollution, fraud, and bribery, cause far greater and farther reaching public harm than do more visible street crimes. The result is hundreds of deaths and hundreds of thousands of injuries every year, only a portion of which are even reported.

Typically, however, these activities are not constructed as crime. Elite deviance is normalized and elites are provided a range of excuses by which their activities are obscured or reconstructed as something other than criminal or deviant acts. The reconstruction of elite crimes and deviance as normal, acceptable, or even legitimate parts of "the costs of doing business" or "business as usual" is an effect of power. It is part of the process of hegemony, the construction of elite interests as the common good, and the manufacture of consent. Elite crime and deviance rarely results in criminal labelling. This is true even where corporate actions lead to massive and wide ranging harms, as in mining disasters or factory fires. There is usually no prosecution and rarely any jail time.

The first ideological trick by which elite deviance is normalized and excused is the notion of profit. This has already been discussed in Chapter 8. Using the term profit to describe what is actually a theft, the theft of surplus value, excuses a massive transfer of wealth upward, out of working class communities and into private control for the benefit of capital. In this way, the enormous day-to-day looting of wealth is rendered acceptable. What is called profit is really exploitation. It should be identified as such. Imagine if in place of the term profit, the term exploitation was used in public discussions and debates. This would shift the way society viewed the issue. If on the news a report that said the profits of national companies was up, reported instead that exploitation by national companies was up, or theft by national companies was up, people would respond much differently. At the very least, the conversation should start by calling it what it really is. Not profit, which sounds positive, but theft, which has a rather different connotation. This is perhaps the only case in which a theft of grand scale is allowed a different name to obscure or cover up what it actually is. Perhaps shoplifting should be called product testing. Break and enter could be called visiting. Only elite crimes are given such positive references with which to cloak themselves. This is a sleight of hand that covers up, indeed encourages, one of the greatest ongoing thefts in human history.

The second ideological mechanism by which elite deviance and criminality is excused and elite perpetrators left off the hook, is through the misuse of the term "accident" to describe acts and outcomes that are in no way, accidental. Both media and criminal justice system members report elite wrongdoing as accidents when, in fact, the events in question could have been foreseen and avoided — thus were not at all accidental in character. The use of the term accident removes blame from those actually responsible and presents acts with predictable outcomes as random occurrences or acts of nature or flukes that could not have been expected. Yet when one looks at the specific details of most of these events, one finds that they are reasonably expected, even high probability outcomes of the actions in question that led to harm. If an employer or manager sends an employee into an unventilated space known to be filled with toxic fumes and without proper breathing equipment and the worker is fatally overcome by fumes and dies, that is not an accident. It is a reasonably-expected outcome, a likely outcome. This scenario actually occurred in Langley, British Columbia resulting in the deaths of three workers. If a boss asks a worker to use a piece of machinery that is not properly maintained and the worker is injured or killed, that is not an accident, it is a reasonably-expected outcome. If a corporate executive orders toxic waste dumped in a local stream and wildlife and people in the community become ill or die, that is not an accident, it is a reasonably-expected outcome. Yet such activities occur on an everyday basis in capitalist societies and are identified as accidents rather than what they are — criminal acts.

The third ideological mechanism deployed to excuse elite wrongdoing is the notion of externality. An externality refers to a cost of doing business for a private interest that is offloaded onto the public. Businesses reap the profit from their activities and simultaneously shift the cost of doing business onto society, the local community, or the workers. If a company decides to cut costs by failing to build proper waste treatment facilities and instead dumps their wastes in the environment; the costs of cleanup, rescue of animals, or treatment of the ill are borne, not be the company responsible, but by society at large. That is an externality. If companies do not put proper safety equipment in their workplaces and workers are injured or made ill, the cost of medical treatment and care for workers who are harmed is an externality. The company does not pay for it. You and I do through our medical care system. Once again, elite wrongdoers are absolved of blame and treated with impunity by governments, media, and criminal justice systems. Responsibility is not placed where it rightly should be and is instead shifted away from the elite wrongdoers who should be held to account.

White Collar Crime: The Work of Edwin Sutherland

Criminology has, throughout its history, given most of its attention to street crime rather than suite crime. It has, therefore, let non-elites and perpetrators of large scale social harm off the hook while reinforcing the notion that the proper subjects of crime and punishment are the working classes and the poor. Indeed, into the twenty-first century, there are many criminology departments that lacked courses on corporate crime or elite deviance, while offering numerous courses on various street crimes such as gangs or drug use.

The first criminologist to press for the systematic study of elite crime and deviance was Edwin Sutherland, who we met earlier with regard to differential association theory. During the 1939 meetings of the American Sociological Association, Sutherland implored criminologists to turn their attention to crimes committed by those who enjoyed high status within society.

Criminologists must avoid the temptation of always focusing on visible and accessible street crimes and take the time to investigate less visible, but more socially damaging elite crimes. It was Sutherland who introduced the term, widely used popularly today, of "white collar crime." For Sutherland, the definition of crime must be expanded, to take in activities that have been overlooked. Even more, criminologists must not let prestige and respectability interfere with honest investigation and assessment of elite activities.

As Sutherland notes in discussing differential association theory, close elite networks provide venues and opportunities to learn deviance and to rationalize it as acceptable or "simply doing business." If one wants to find real crime, and massively damaging activities, do not waste time in the subcultural haunts of the poor and working classes, the burlesque halls, gin joints, or hobo jungles of Chicago School research. The crimes "uncovered" in those sites are easy to find and really amount to peanuts. If you want to find real wrongdoing, exponentially worse in impact and consequence than the street crimes of the working class subcultures; go to the spaces and venues of the elites — the yacht clubs, business schools, country clubs, and private establishments. There you will find large scale criminal activity with repercussions for hundreds of thousands of people. These are the "big picture" crimes.

Criminologists will have to work harder to access white collar crime because it often takes place behind closed doors in private settings behind walls of security. Researchers will confront numerous gatekeepers, including high-priced lawyers and public relations firms that make the task of research difficult. They must not be dissuaded from continuing the work of criminology on the basis of convenience.

In order to shift criminological thinking about crime and deviance, and the harmful activities engaged by elites on a daily basis, Sutherland identified a series of white collar crimes. This list was presented in the midst of the Great Depression and brink of World War II at a time when the public was being implored to rally behind corporate and political endeavours.

The first harm, in the language of the day, can be categorized as stings and swindles. These activities involve the use of deception to steal from someone. An example from Sutherland's era might include door-to-door vacuum salespeople who pressure sell what is supposedly a great labour-saving device but actually delivers a piece of junk that breaks down on first real use. Late night cable television provides a whole range of stings and swindles. Paid programming that sells hip hop weight loss programs, male enhancement supplements, super knives, and fake jewellery are all contemporary examples of stings and swindles. So too, from a non-business perspective, are televangelists who ask people to send donations to be prayed for or to receive a (fake) religious artifact.

The second activity is, again in the language of the day, chiselling. This involves the subtle cheating of customers. It includes altering products, as when additives are used to stretch more expensive ingredients, such as the use of alum in bread to cut grain costs. It can also involve the use of shoddy ingredients or products, such as lower-grade woods used in condo construction. It also includes mislabelling of products. In Canada, for example, there has been no legislation requiring food companies to identify all of the ingredients in their product. Often companies will use corporate created names to refer to groupings of unnamed ingredients. Such is the case in the labelling of "lemon pulp" in lemonade concentrate. Lemon pulp actually refers to a chemical mix that includes such unnamed ingredients as formaldehyde.

The third white collar crime is the exploitation of one's institutional position. This involves using one's institutional power or authority to take advantage of people, typically within an organization. It can include employers pressuring employees for sexual favors with the threat of job loss if they refuse.

The fourth activity involves influence peddling and bribery. In this case, executives and power holders sell power, influence, and insider information to outsiders. Influence peddling is a regular feature of economic and political life in liberal democracies. Much of the lobbying industry is more accurately labelled influence peddling or bribery. That it is not, is an effect of power or hegemony. Examples recently include the secret meetings between former Prime Minister Brian Mulroney and an operative of Airbus during which envelopes of money allegedly exchanged hands at a time when the government had been considering contracts for air service vehicles.

The fifth activity involves embezzlement or employee fraud. This includes using one's position to steal company funds or property. It can include the theft of monies from employee pension funds, leaving thousands impoverished in their retirement.

The sixth white collar crime identified by Sutherland is client fraud. This can include a range of activities by which clients have money taken from them by an organization they trust.

The final category is a catch-all category of corporate crime. This involves willful violation of the laws that otherwise restrict corporations. It consists of any socially injurious act that is committed by corporations or individual operatives in pursuing their specific business interests. This last category, though, shows the limitation of Sutherland's early approach. Notably, many harmful activities engaged in by corporations and executives are not in violation of established laws. One of the real problems is that so much of corporate deviance and harm are not criminalized. They are accepted or overlooked. In addition, it is difficult to establish "willfulness" if the media and state automatically identify elite harmful activities as "accidents."

Still, Sutherland's work made important contributions to shift criminological focus away from street crimes of non-elites and toward the suite crime of economic and political elites. His work should be recognized as a significant innovation. Others, including sociologists like C. Wright Mills, have worked to develop the analysis in both deeper and more expansive ways. Mills work on the power elite remains among the most useful contributions to analyses of social power in contemporary capitalist societies.

The Power Elite and the Military-Industrial Complex

The often hidden connections between state, corporate, and military actors, and their roles in determining social development, have long been concerns within modern industrial societies. These alliances involve circuits of contracts, finances, resources, and personnel between institutions, including those of state representatives, defense contractors, arms manufacturers, and military leadership. Of much concern, these networks are typically informal and operate behind the scenes through personal relationships, lobbying efforts, campaign work, and professional associations. Thus, they raise important questions about the real nature of decision making, and the distribution and structure of power, within contemporary liberal democracies. This nexus of power holders, and its transformation of society, has been called the military-industrial complex.

Contemporary military machinery, highly mechanized, integrated with systems of information technologies and computerization, have required new regimes of production and capital accumulation. Militarization extends beyond weapons to establish systems of research, development, production, and deployment that rely upon extensive integrated state-corporate networks. These systems are based on complex divisions of labour, specialized knowledge, and advanced technological apparatuses. In order to maintain advanced military production, ongoing mass infrastructures are required, rather than ad hoc facilities that might emerge to meet specific war needs. Countries with major military forces have been compelled to establish permanent war economies, ongoing structures responsible for the regular production of war equipment. This requirement has provided the context for durable state-corporate-military alliances as growing sections of national economies are given over to military development. State-corporate-military alliances shape priorities of research and development, scientific investigations and university teaching, through funding, research grants, and endowed university chairs. There are concerns that military research comes at the expense of other research.

The last sixty years have seen a massive and broad transformation in the size and scope of military operations and expenditures in countries such as the U.S. Beginning with the First World War, the U.S. shifted from a peacetime military, which was relatively small and relied upon militia and reserves in times of war, to a constantly growing standing army. The U.S. never fully demobilized after World War I and the total mobilization that accompanied the U.S. involvement in World War II, along with the decimation of European and Japanese forces, left the U.S. with the largest, most advanced military on the planet by war's end. In the post-war period, the competition and distrust between the remaining global powers, the U.S. and Soviet Union, encouraged the growth and development of military equipment and infrastructures in the U.S. Military buildup during the Cold War cost taxpayers an average of around 6% of GDP (Napoleoni 2010). At the height of the Vietnam War, the military apparatus impacted the public treasury to the tune of 9.3% of GDP (Napoleoni 2010). That war also exhausted U.S. gold reserves leading eventually to the end of the gold-exchange standard, which has resulted in monetary crises (and associated food crises) related to financial speculation, which has, in turn, deeply, negatively, impacted poor people globally.

It is estimated that current military expenditures in the U.S. make up almost half of the value of arms purchases each year (SIPRI 2010). U.S. defense spending is twice as much as the combined total of the 15 nations with the next highest military expenditures (Napoleoni 2010). By the middle of 2007, U.S. public debt represented around 40% of GDP and this was due largely to military expenditures (Napoleoni 2010). Between 2004 and 2008 the annual budget of the Pentagon grew from $420 billion (U.S.) to $700 billion (U.S.) (Napoleoni 2010). One source suggests that world expenditures on military sources reached $1.531 trillion (U.S.) in 2009 (SIPRI 2010). Of this, almost $712 billion (U.S.) was paid by the U.S. Other sources suggest that total U.S. spending on military sources is close to $1 trillion (U.S.) when all materials and sources, including those outside Defense Department budgets are taken into account (Higgs 2007). Economic consequences of the war economy include public debt, inflation, and recession (Napoleoni 2010). There is concern that such military-driven policies, along with associated cuts to corporate taxes, could lead the U.S. to bankruptcy.

The term military-industrial-complex gained popular notice following its use during the Farewell Address of President Dwight D. Eisenhower in 1960. In his speech, Eisenhower warned citizens to be vigilant against the accumulation of power, whether sought or unsought, by the military-industrial-complex. Noting the rise of a mechanized standing army, which was different in size and character from a citizens' army or yeoman's militia, Eisenhower raised concerns about the influence on democratic practice and the domination of social matters by corporate-military considerations posed by the presence of a permanent army, and military infrastructures, that made up a significant portion of the national economy.

As Eisenhower noted, the decision to build tanks, bombs, or fighter jets is not simply a matter of military, or even economic, policy regarding state expenditures. More important, the decision to build and purchase armaments is a social policy decision. It is simultaneously a decision not to fund housing, health care, education, or agriculture. Policies that benefit the military and industrial contractors change the character of society as a whole. They define the type of society that will develop over the course of generations. A society that prioritizes the needs of state-corporate-military networks will not be able to fulfill other, more pressing, social needs. The result will be a society driven by undemocratic structures that fails to meet the needs of its citizenry. It will become an oligarchy of economic and political powerholders rather than a democracy; and social needs of the many will be made secondary to the financial interests of the few. Eisenhower's address was a profound warning, generally considered to be the most significant presidential speech on economic matters of the last fifty years.

An early analysis of the mutually reinforcing networks among corporations, the state, and military was provided by the anarchist Daniel Guérin in his book, *Fascism and Big Business* in 1936. One of the first, and most significant, early analyses of political economic structures of fascism, Guérin's work details the role of fascist governments in rapid industrialization and the central place played by arms manufacturers in the modernization of industry and new forms of capital accumulation through state partnerships with private capital. Guérin defines the state-corporate-military associations under fascism as informal coalitions made up of groups from each sector that act behind the scenes to establish and maintain policies and practices beneficial to the network. These practices and policies are centered upon the development and wielding of high concentrations of weaponry, the maintenance of colonial markets, and conceptions of domestic affairs dominated by strategic military perspectives rather than social policy perspectives. Thus, social problems, such as unemployment, poverty, or dissent, are viewed as strategic issues to be addressed through military responses. Notably, Guérin identifies the members of the network as sharing more than material interests. They also share psychological and moral views of society. Significantly, these networks wield power in a manner that is beyond public view.

Perhaps the most significant and influential analysis of the emergent state-corporate-military alliance in the U.S. came from critical sociologist C. Wright Mills. In his work, still relevant almost sixty years after its publication, *The Power Elite* (1956) Mills argued that a new strata of political, corporate, and military leaders have become the real social and political powerholders in society, not elected government representatives. This nexus of elites holds mutual reinforcing economic and political interests based on growth of arms manufacturing and military infrastructures. Notably, Mills suggested that these elites function as an unseen government that operates beyond popular view or democratic control. Even more, the power elite are not associated with any one political party, whether Republican or Democrat, and they cannot be voted out of office. In any event, even those members who are office holders will simply take up positions within another organization, typically corporate, within the network. It was Mills' work that most influenced Eisenhower's discussion of the military-industrial-complex.

For Mills, the power elite shared not only economic interests but a common view of society. Their perspective is based on four characteristics. First, they hold to a "military metaphysic" in which social and cultural issues are viewed militaristically. Thus, poverty might be addressed through a "war on poverty" rather than other, more socially oriented, means. Second, they possess a shared class identity in which they view themselves as privileged actors who are beyond the law. Third, they enjoy interchangeability within the network. They hold overlapping positions and readily move between institutional structures when necessary. An example would be a politician who moves between corporate boards and directorships and public office or government administration and back again, as in the case of Vice President Dick Cheney and Halliburton. Fourth, elite members socialize recruits to be part of the network and advance them as they show their willingness and capacity to promote the elite worldview. For Mills, the significant lesson is the way in which such alliances can arise within democratic societies and subvert those democracies. According to Mills, this threat was as real in post-war U.S. society, with its rapid militarization, and advanced mechanical weaponry, as it had been in Nazi Germany. Mills' work influenced the discussions of state-corporate-military alliances for generations.

More recently, critical criminologists have examined the ongoing interplay between government agencies and private capital, which owns and operates means of production as part of the regular, if illegitimate, functioning of capitalist economies. Harmful activities that emerge as part of this interplay are referred to as state-corporate crime by criminologists such as Kramer and Michalowski (1991; 2006). Kramer and Michalowski define state-corporate crime as "illegal or socially injurious actions that occur when one or more institutions of political governance pursue a goal in direct co operation with one or more institutions of economic production and distribution (quoted in O'Grady 2007, 153). The work of Kramer and Michalowski has helped to shift criminological study of elite deviance away from studies of the state, capital, and military as atomized institutions, shifting the emphasis toward networked practices and ongoing alliances within and between institutions. In more recent analyses, Kramer and Michalowski have examined military events such as the Iraq war and occupation after September 11, 2001, as an example of state-corporate crime (2005). They provide an analysis of these events, which they define as criminal, that situates the war and occupation as part of broader organizational deviance. Their work offers an integrated model or organizational analysis that looks at historical as well as contemporary state-corporate-military structures.

A Case of Elite Deviance: Shipping and Pollution

Marine pollution and climate change are recognized as two of the four primary threats to the world's oceans, along with over-fishing and habitat destruction. Shipping stands with fishing as the most intensive human uses of the planet's oceans. Shipping is a major contributor to marine pollution as well as contributing to climate change. Shipping is a major source of water and air pollution. Among the pollution and waste resulting from shipping are: emissions of air contaminants, including sulphur dioxide, carbon dioxide, carbon monoxide, and hydrocarbons; chemical wastes released as part of regular operational processes, including industrial cleaning agents used in the upkeep of ships' mechanical operations as well as household chemicals used in cleaning human quarters; releases of solid waste materials, including onboard garbage; the intentional dumping of hazardous wastes; release of untreated or improperly treated sewage; and accidental spills of harmful materials, including chemical and oil spills. In addition to marine spills and pollution related to shipping, shipping has also contributed to the spread of invasive species through the discharge of ballast water containing living organisms.

In the twenty-first century, shipping is a massive and fully global enterprise. With corporate globalization and the expansion of multinational trading regimes, the use of ocean-going vessels to transport freight has increased, and continues to grow. Ocean-based shipping is now the means of transport for something on the order of 90% of world trade (Talouli, n.d.). It is clear that without the use of ocean-going transport, corporate globalization could not have developed in the broad manner that it has and would not have secured the economic rationality from which it currently profits.

Estimates suggest that there are approximately 85,000 commercial ships registered within flag States (Talouli, n.d.). These vessels transport approximately 5,400 million tonnes of cargo across the world's oceans each year (Talouli, n.d.). Contemporary shipping practices are made up of a wide range of ship types of various sizes, ranging from car ferries to super tankers and container ships. Shipping is categorized as domestic, international, or transit (shipping that passes through a region without calling at any port).

Most ocean freighters are driven by diesel powered engines. Pollution from diesel fuel represents one of the most dangerous sources of air contamination. Residual fuel used in powering shipping vessels contains sulfur levels almost 2,000 times greater than U.S. law allows for other diesel engines (Vidal 2009). It is estimated that emissions related to shipping contribute to almost 60,000 deaths globally each year and contribute additionally to a range of respiratory ailments (Corbett and Winebrake 2007a; 2007b). Effects are pronounced along the coastal regions on major trade routes (Corbett and Winebrake 2007a; 2007b).

It is also suggested that ocean-going vessels account for around 3% of global climactic change emissions worldwide. Shipping is responsible for an estimated 1.12 billion metric tonnes of carbon dioxide. This represents almost 4.5% of all global emissions of carbon dioxide, the primary greenhouse gas. The shipping industry globally is responsible for more greenhouse gas emissions annually than all countries on the planet except for China, India, Japan, Russia, and the United States. One container shipping vessel is estimated to produce the greenhouse gas emissions of 50,000 cars (Vidal 2009).

Garbage has proven as harmful to marine life as chemical and oil spills. The material that makes up most of marine garbage — and the one that is the most harmful and poses the most lasting impact — is plastic. Some plastics can take close to 500 years to dissolve in the oceans. It is estimated that there are around eight million items of marine litter entering the oceans each day (UNEP 2006). It is suggested that around 60% of this comes from shipping, whether intentionally or unintentionally (UNEP 2006). The known total of plastic litter floating on every square mile of ocean is more than 46,000 pieces (UNEP 2006). The impacts of plastic waste are severe. Plastics can contribute to habitat loss and the fouling of ecosystems as well as posing a fatal threat to specific animals which become entrapped in, or injured by the waste matter.

Each year approximately 1 million sea birds, 100,000 sea mammals, and untold numbers of fish are killed by plastic waste (UNEP 2006). In addition, Marine debris has associated harms such as posing navigational hazards to other vessels. Some of these hazards have resulted in the capsizing of vessels and the loss of human life.

Another growing problem is the issue of invasive species released from the ballast water of ocean-going shipping vessels. These invasive species have caused significant environmental damage to a variety of ecosystems, as in cases of the introduction of North Pacific Starfish in Australia and the Zebra Mussels and Green Crabs in Canada. The development of larger ships and the expansion of shipping trade have contributed to the substantial spread of invasive species transported in ballast water. In some cases, ecosystems have been dramatically transformed through the introduction of invasive plant species from ballast water into new environments, as in the case of purple loosestrife in Canada.

There are significant social repercussions resulting from shipping waste. The impacts of environmental waste are directly connected with issues of poverty in human communities. Poor people and communities are most negatively affected by damage to food sources or loss of resources. They are also most negatively impacted economically or financially by harm done to resources, particularly within subsistence economies. Poor people also have fewer resources available to deal with the effects of exposure to waste and toxic substances.

People whose diets consist of regular consumption of aquatic species can be threatened. Health impacts can be particularly severe for women and children. Fat soluble toxins accumulate in women's bodies, due to higher fat levels, posing serious health risks. These risks can be passed to children through breast milk. Children are particularly vulnerable to contaminants such as lead or mercury.

Unfortunately, few steps have been taken to address shipping-related waste and pollution. Some global measures include the Convention on the Prevention of Marine Pollution by Dumping of Wastes and Other Matter, 1972; the Basel Convention on the Control of Transboundary Movements of Hazardous Wastes and their Disposal, 1989; the International Convention for the Prevention of Pollution from Ships, 1973 and its amended Protocol of 1978; and the Rotterdam Convention on the Prior Informed Consent Procedure for Certain Hazardous Chemicals and Pesticides in International Trade, 1998. With the centrality of shipping transport within the global economy, it is clear that community and workplace organizing, rather than industry initiatives, will be required to improve the situation.

Conclusion

Most of harmful elite activities go entirely undetected and are not even researched by members of criminal justice organizations or by criminologists. Corporate regulators are understaffed and underfunded where they exist at all. At the same time, public calls go out for increased community policing of the streets and more bylaws that penalize street crimes.

An overall effect is that the public remain less aware of and less vigilant of elite crime and deviance. More people in Canada and the U.S. risk death and injury simply going to work to try and put a roof over their heads and food on the table, than they do of being assaulted or killed in a street crime. The most dangerous person in anyone's life may well be their employer. Yet, despite the facts of workplace death and injury and their more regular occurrence compared to assault and murder, industrial fatalities and injuries are not at the forefront of public consciousness in the way that street crimes are. Industrial harms are not recognized largely by state policy or discourse which focuses on street crimes. The mass media do not investigate or emphasize the tragedies of industrial damage, except in occasional extreme cases, which are generally presented as unfortunate "accidents." This is in marked contrast to sensational news accounts presented every day involving street crimes.

Many government officials are drawn from the ranks of corporate executives, lawyers, and accountants. These are the same people then charged with regulating the corporate enterprises, and friends and colleagues, for which they have dutifully spent their working lives. Corporate officials are part of powerful networks, including prestigious university faculties, professional schools, exclusive clubs, high priced law firms, and public relations departments.

In fact, much of elite crime and deviance has been made to legislatively disappear. This is made to happen through a variety of acts by governments. First, there is the repeal of already existing laws. In this way, many acts of elite wrongdoing are simply decriminalized with the stroke of a pen. Laws against media concentration and monopoly offer recent examples. Second, there is deregulation and the cancelling of criminal and civil laws and practices that acted as checks against extremes of elite harm, as in food or health and safety regulations. Third, there is downsizing and the destruction of government regulatory capacities. This occurs through the layoff and firing of regulators and the cutting of resources for remaining regulators. It also occurs through policies of self-regulation, allowing elite entities to police themselves. Notably such options are not available to those who might be engaged in street crimes.

CHAPTER 12

Moral Regulation: Panic, Control, and the Construction of Social Problems

Critical theorists suggest that in stratified societies, the norms of elite groups are typically constructed as being legitimate, common, or shared. Elite needs are presented as "the common good" and dominant morality reflects the interests and concerns of elites. Critics ask, whose values are viewed as normal and whose are viewed as pathological? They also ask, who is regulated and who does the regulating?

State Morality

The state legislation of morality is perhaps most closely associated with theocratic states or governments in which morals derived from religious beliefs coincide with and are expressed in state policies, legislation, and punishment regimes. Under such regimes, there is no separation of church and state and, indeed, the head of state is often the head of the dominant religious organization.

During the medieval period in Europe, monarchs asserted their right to rule and establish laws on the basis of divine right in which their power derived from their nearness to God. The nobility placed themselves at the top of the "great chain of being," with the serfs over whom they ruled being closer to base animals and therefore, unfit to rule. Only the nobility were created in the image of God, indeed they proclaimed that they had been touched by God. This ideology was used to justify the absolute authority of the monarch whose power had been conferred directly as an act of God's will and was therefore unquestionable and could not be challenged by the people. The dictates of the monarch, an unconditional authority, legislated morality as an expression of God's will on earth. Only God could judge a monarch's behaviour, thus any rebellion or disobedience against the monarch would be an act of sacrilege.

In China, rulers referred to the Mandate of Heaven to justify their rule. In a manner similar to divine right in Europe, the Mandate legitimized rulership through reference to divine will. Under this perspective, ruling morality was legislated as divine will on Earth. Unlike divine right in Europe, the Mandate could transfer away from unfit or unjust rulers and did not grant unconditional authority. In addition, it did not mandate that rulers be restricted to nobility.

In the current period, theocratic governments continue to unify state and religious authority. Modern theocratic states operate in several countries including Iran, Oman, Saudi Arabia, and Yemen. Legislation in Egypt is vetted for its agreement with religious teachings. The Vatican City represents another form of theocratic government. Some suggest that the Israeli state is another form of theocracy. Others have warned that the U.S., particularly the influence of fundamentalist Protestantism, has drifted precariously close to being a theocracy.

With the emergence of liberal democratic governments and the assertion of separation between church and state as a principle of democratic government, ruling authorities have used different approaches to legislate morality beyond direct appeals to religious teachings. Practices within liberal democratic capitalist systems are sometimes identified as bourgeois morality or moral regulation (Foucault 1975; 1976).

Commentators note that the modern state has grown through increasing involvement in growing areas of social life, from working activity to consumption practices to sexuality, childrearing, and education, among others. Among the most familiar contemporary examples include legislation against drinking and driving, growing penalties against smoking, and longstanding prohibitions against recreational drug use. In these cases, where there is much social debate and conflict over the question of legislation, the contested character of moral perspectives in diverse, democratic societies is clear. Instances such as the failed attempt to enforce prohibition against alcohol in the U.S. show how tenuous the state legislation of morality can be and how steadfastly it might be opposed. State legislation has made use of new intellectual practices and disciplines from medicine to psychology to social work.

One of the issues in which moral regulation and the legislation of morality have been exhibited throughout the course of capitalist modernity involves the regulation of poverty and the development of the corporate work ethic. In the early stages of capitalist development and industrialization, liberal democratic states developed punishments targeting poor and homeless people simply for being poor and homeless. Various Poor Laws were used to arrest and detain poor people who were then made to labour in state work camps. Such laws persist in the twenty-first century as laws such as the Safe Streets Acts in Ontario and British Columbia, Canada give police the power to arrest people for street survival acts such as panhandling. Robert Miles argues that the model for contemporary practices of class inferiorization began in sixteenth century Europe as discrimination against the poor, especially beggars. This was part of a "civilizing project" designed to establish and legitimize a social system of emerging power differentials. Feudal rulers changed their behaviors initially by making their bodily functions more private. This behavioral shift allowed them to contrast their "refined" activities with those of the "inferior" people whom they ruled (Miles 1993, 90-97). People in the business and industrial classes imitated this "civilized" behavior, presenting their prudent values as inherited rather than socially constructed. Miles suggests that this civilizing project encompassed forms of domestic racism in Europe, in which privileged Europeans portrayed themselves as superior to the people they ruled, that provided the foundation for colonial racism. These practices are reflected in contemporary policies of citizenship and immigration controls. Within capitalist culture, the identifying characteristics of a good person become constructed as rejecting idleness and unproductive pleasures and attending to one's business with thrift and industriousness. Poverty is constructed as evidence of moral weakness or lack of character, which the state is expected to discourage.

Moral Panics and Folk Devils

One of the key sociological concepts developed to explain processes of moral regulation is the notion of moral panics. This concept comes from the work of critical criminologist Stanley Cohen and his influential work *Folk Devils and Moral Panics* (1973). Cohen's early study examined the way in which a minor conflict between two youth subcultural groups became blown out of proportion and led to legislation that punished youth, even if they only displayed the styles of the subcultures but were not members. Through his research,

Cohen uncovered the active parts played by business people and commercial interests in targeting the subcultures for punishment based, not on the activities of the groups involved, but on concern for profits and lost business posed by the mere presence of the groups, who were believed to scare away mainstream customers. Cohen also noted the activities of local police who wanted more tools for acting against subcultures that they disagreed with.

Cohen developed the term "moral panic" to describe and explain the processes by which a group of people, typically elites or more privileged groups, react negatively to the behaviors, cultural practices, or styles of another group, usually non-elites and often subcultures or minority group members. The dominant group uses mass media to publicize its concerns and convince others that they should be concerned as well. Through the mobilization of fear and contempt through the media, the dominant group is able to construct the targeted group as a public threat that must be regulated. The usual outcome of a moral panic is the passing of legislation prohibiting, restricting, or criminalizing the targeted group and/or specific activities associated with it.

Notably, the targeted group is usually involved in activities that are not socially harmful. They might be involved in nuisance activities, activities that inconvenience people, or activities of self harm, but not socially dangerous acts. Usually the targeted groups or their activities only bother specific people or groups rather than society more broadly. But, crucially, the groups that are bothered by the targeted group and/or its activities are powerful enough to make public their concerns and mobilize social resources on their behalf. Through connections with media and politicians, they can make their particular interests become social or common interests.

The targeted group is identified by Cohen as a folk devil. The folk devils are made subjects of rumor and defamation campaigns, starting at local levels but spreading through the use of mass media. Examples of contemporary folk devils include hip hop and punk subcultures, homeless people, riot grrrls or young feminists, ravers, metal thieves, and drug addicts.

In the case of the Safe Streets Act and criminalization of squeegeeing and panhandling in Ontario and British Columbia, one can see processes very similar to those outlined by Cohen. In these cases, concerns about squeegeeing and panhandling, as potentially harmful activities, were raised not by the general public but by business people and merchants worried about commercial losses because of the mere presence of homeless people near their shops. They mobilized media to demonize homeless people and construct them as objects of fear and contempt, and then lobbied governments to respond to the constructed fear with legislation. Thus, the media and governments, locally and provincially, were played as tools for private business interests to negatively impact homeless people who should have received public support instead. The only concern was a private concern to drive homeless people out of specific commercial areas in cities like Toronto, Ottawa, Victoria, and Vancouver.

Moral regulation can be examined in other contexts. The following two sections examine two areas around which there has been much discussion, debate, disagreement, and moralizing recently.

Steroids in Sports

Steroids in sports first came to international prominence during the World Weightlifting Championships of 1954, when Soviet athletes dominated most of the weight classes in each event. Upon learning that the Soviet athletes had received testosterone injections, U.S. team physician Dr. John Ziegler set about to devise something to keep his own athletes competitive. The result was Dianabol or Methandrostenolone, an anabolic steroid developed by Ziegler and the Ciba pharmaceutical company.

By the late 1960s, East German athletes became a major force in world competitions following a government recommendation that steroids be administered to all national team members in a program to increase national pride through global athletic success.

Steroids were of less concern during the Cold War as the western countries felt the need to compete with the Soviet countries as part of a broader ideological struggle to show the supremacy of social systems. At the same time, the rumored use of steroids by the Soviet bloc teams, like the claim that their athletes were actually professionals, served to justify similar activities by western countries.

In 1968, the first official complaint about steroid use was lodged by the World Health Organization over the widespread prescription of steroids in poorer countries, including Kenya and Jamaica. Prior to the 1972 Olympics, the International Olympic Committee issued a ban on anabolic steroids and those games saw the first athlete caught under the ban, American swimmer Rick DeMont.

Over the intervening decades, steroids became a major part of nearly all of competitive sports, from amateur sports like track and field, swimming and cycling to professional sports like football and baseball. Notably, the great increase in steroid use coincided with the period, beginning in the late-1980s, when corporate sponsorship and massive television contracts increased exponentially the financial rewards available even to "amateur" athletics. Indeed, this period saw the Olympics opened up to professional, star athletes. With the exception of high profile cases like the expulsion of Canadian gold medal sprinter Ben Johnson, there was little public mobilization against steroid use, which was viewed as a matter of internal regulation by the official sporting federations and major leagues involved.

The broad social concern with steroids in North American sports grew following President George W. Bush's State of the Union address in 2004. During that speech, Bush identified steroids as a societal danger and called upon sporting bodies to eliminate them from their games.

Many perceive the issue to be little more than a moral panic, like the drug wars of the 1980s and 1990s, initiated by politicians as a means of exerting social regulation, especially over youth. Thus, concern for youth is presented as a central message in appeals to end steroid use in sports. In terms of safety, however, it can be noted that the sports themselves, especially football, are far more dangerous than steroids. The number of deaths from college and professional football is believed to be 50 to 100 times higher than any known number of deaths from steroids.

The mainstream media treatment of baseball's home run record-holder Barry Bonds is another case that reveals aspects of the late culture wars. For some, the harsh focus on Bonds, who has been constructed unanimously as a reviled figure, is an expression of racism. The media campaign against a top-level African-American athlete, perhaps the best ever at his sport, is compared to the relatively soft treatment of even admitted users of banned substances who happen to be white, such as Jason Giambi, Andy Pettite and, prior to his embarrassing performance before Senate, Roger Clemens.

For some, the moral outrage directed at players as the primary figures in steroids debates, rather than team owners and managers or league officials, is a significant and telling aspect of the culture wars. That owners have been given relatively little attention or scorn, while also shouldering less responsibility for the growth of steroids within their sports, is taken as a sign that corporate leaders are not subject to the same acts of criticism or punishment as the people, even highly paid people, who work for them. It can be asked why players, almost exclusively, have been put through the degradation ceremonies of government hearings, while owners have been given a platform to proclaim their moral indignation and commitment to improvements. This inequality of treatment also extends to administrators such as Gary Bettman of the National Hockey League and Bud Selig of Major League Baseball, who act on behalf of owners to negotiate collective bargaining agreements and ensure profitability. Bettman and Selig both chose to ignore steroid use for years while watching revenues increase, yet they have shouldered little of the blame for the growth of steroids in their sports. This, despite the fact that managing performance standards was primarily their responsibility. It is perhaps no coincidence that major league baseball players, even more than football players where the use of banned substances is still believed to be rampant, have received the most sustained negative attention given that their union, the Major League Baseball Players' Association, is the strongest in all professional sports, the only major sport union to successfully refuse a cap on players' salaries.

Once again corporate profit tells the story. Baseball revenues, attendance, and memorabilia sales have increased since the Mark McGwire and Sammy Sosa home run race in 1998. Yet a bottle of androstenedione was found in McGwire's locker during the record-breaking run and McGwire openly admitted to using the substance. The return to popularity of baseball, desperately needed following the cancellation of the World Series in 1994 as part of MLB's attempt to break the player's union, is widely attributed to the increase in home runs, led by spectacle such as the McGwire-Sosa duel, which is, in part, a result of steroid use. MLB teams that later proclaimed their concern with steroids had no trouble accepting the major revenue increases enjoyed for most of a decade during the "steroids era." Their concern really only piqued when the potential costs of negative publicity threatened to harm revenues. Even more likely, motivation came from the threat that MLB would lose its anti-trust exemption, which would throw the league open to government regulation and allow for greater competition from outside leagues.

Video Games

Video games have been at the center of cultural debates since the earliest days of electric pinball machines in the late-1930s. Fearing the use of machines in gambling and connections with organized crime networks, Mayor LaGuardia of New York City illegalized pinball machines, scrapping their materials for use in war production. With the development of video games as a multi-billion dollar industry since the late-1970s, concerns over their place in society, and their potentially harmful impacts, especially on youth, have escalated. Video games have been attacked by commentators on the left and right for their supposedly anti-social character and for the risk they pose in distortion of the social and cultural values of young people. Wildly popular games such as Grand Theft Auto, which valorize theft, abuse, and killings are presented as contributors to a deterioration of civic values, morals, and social responsibility. For defenders of video games, they represent playful and harmless fantasy and actually contribute to social networks and sociability among the youth who play them. At most they reflect, rather than constitute, cultural values.

Initial concerns over video games focused on the supposedly unsavory environment of video arcades which were publically constructed as potential sites of youth degeneracy. Arcades were presented, with little supporting evidence, as dens of drug trafficking and use, sexual experimentation, and juvenile delinquency. In reality, these wild accusations spoke to an underlying fear of arcades as centers of youth autonomy. These were spaces composed almost exclusively of youth from which adults were largely excluded, socially and culturally as well as physically. These spaces were largely free from adult supervision and surveillance, and relied upon the judgments and interactions of youth themselves. Arcades became the pool halls and rock clubs that had formed the sites of adult fears of adolescents in previous generations. Early public responses to video arcades included the passing of civic bylaws and ordinances restricting the hours and conditions of operation of video arcades.

With the emergence of home entertainment systems and the move of video games from the arcade to the living room, new concerns emerged. These largely centered around the use of time by children and youth. Because parents could now directly observe their children's video game activities, the amount of time spent playing video games joined a concern with the content of those games. These fears were reinforced by early psychological studies suggesting that youth preferred the virtual companionship of video games to the real companionship of family and friends.

Perhaps the greatest social concern over video games involves the large emphasis games place on violence and aggressive behaviours. Much of video game play involves numerous and varied acts of brutality and plots that involve conquest, domination, and control. While this has been especially the case of the home and computer game markets since the late 1990s and early 2000s, critics note that violence has routinely played a part in video game narratives and actions, since the early arcade games of the 1970s. In addition to open and explicit portrayals of violence, including what might be called sadistic violence in enormously popular games such as Doom or Mortal Combat, critics contend that video games create a social context supporting, reinforcing or even nurturing the dehumanization of people and an instrumental approach to people as obstacles to be overcome. Indeed, acts of violence are typically rewarded in video games through the awarding of points, treasure, or playing time. In addition, success and movement through game levels is often tracked through numbers of kills. Indeed, Retired Lt. Col. David Grossman has argued that the techniques used in video games are the same as those used by the military in training recruits to overcome their ingrained resistance to killing and to transform them into killers. These techniques desensitize recruits into viewing killing as a strategic response rather than an act of moral consequence.

A public panic over violence in video games first emerged in the U.S. in 1976. At the center of the storm was the arcade game Death Race, which involved players racing cars over skeletons that, due to the limited graphics of the day, resembled people. Initial concerns raised by parents eventually gave rise to protest movements to have the game banned. Death Race and the potentially harmful impacts of video game violence were featured in a segment of the television news program *60 Minutes*. While many arcades and stores refused to carry Death Race, the game's manufacturer, Exidy, recorded unprecedented business as a result of the media attention their game received.

Violence in video games became the centerpiece of a moral panic following the massacre at Columbine High School in Littleton, Colorado. The two killers were said to be avid video game players. Following the killings, President Clinton called for a Surgeon General's investigation into the harmful effects of video games on children. Labelling of video games for violence and sexuality and their subjection to a rating system similar to that of movies and music was instituted. Senators Joe Lieberman and Hillary Clinton have since called for a more restrictive ratings system following the issuing of a less severe "Mature" rating for the game Manhunt 2.

Liberal critics have been especially concerned about the impact, whether intended or not, of video games on the development of militaristic tendencies in society and the possible preparation of society for military action through the use of video games. The danger of possible connections between video games and militarism became an issue early in the development of arcade video games. During the mid-1980s, the developer of the popular game Battlezone, a tank simulator using innovative graphics and game play, Ed Rotberg, was approached by the U.S. Army to develop a more realistic version of the game for use in military training programs. Rotberg, who opposed the use of games for military purposes, refused, but his employer Atari proceeded with the project anyway.

Since that time, there has been an extensive interplay between game design and military application. Notably, this has involved a cultural flow in both directions between the gaming and military cultures. It has included the use of video games to train and prepare military personnel as well as the use of images from actual war situations in video games.

Concerns over violence have also addressed issues of violence against women within video games. Notable campaigns have been launched to protest the abuse of women characters within video games, such as the game Double Dragon in which the male characters played by gamers beat prostitutes. Such campaigns have generally served to publicize the game and to increase its play.

Another issue of central concern for video game critics, both liberal and conservative, though for different reasons, involves explicit depictions of sexuality. For liberals, especially liberal feminists, the main issue has been the sexual degradation of women as sex objects or victims of sexual violence within video games. This includes the availability of free online video games that depict women being sexually abused or which involve sexual abuse of women as the game's task. Such game play reinforces other feminist concerns with the diminished status of women within video games, which emphasize male heroes, and the unrealistic portrayal of women's bodies within video games. For conservatives, the main issue has been the widespread availability of sexual imagery within video games, with less regard for specific depictions of women within that imagery. At the same time, campaigns against representations of sex and sexuality within video games and groups involved in those campaigns, such as Women Against Pornography, have brought together liberals and conservatives in sometimes uneasy alliances. Again, however, the emergence of campaigns against sexuality in games, such as those against the game Bachelor Party, have typically served to increase sales or play of the games.

Other issues have involved the treatment of ethnic minorities within video games. African-American and Muslim characters have been disproportionately rendered as villains and enemies or the targets of violence within video games. Since the attacks of September 11, 2001 and the U.S. invasion of Iraq, video games with anti-Muslim and/or pro-invasion themes have proliferated on the Internet.

For proponents of video games, the real culture war over video games is not an ideological one between liberals and conservatives but a generational one between adults, especially those coming of age prior to the 1980s and youth. This argument suggests that even liberal parents who grew up before the 1980s lack the techno-literacy and familiarity with video game media necessary to understand and appreciate the complex, and indeed critically detached, interactions younger generations experience in using and developing video games. There is nothing to compare from earlier times with the electronic environment of the late twentieth and early twenty-first centuries. It was largely the generations that became parents in the 1980s and 1990s that expressed concern with and mobilized against video games.

Defenders of video games note that a lack of understanding of the workings of video games and their general appeal to youth by parents contributed to the sense of fear and worry. At the same time, it is noted that youth do not tend to denigrate their own cultural activities and values or view them deterministically. Such is the purview of outsiders such as parents and other authority figures. Arcades, the fantasy worlds of video games, and the social networks of online role playing games have served as sites of uncertainty and fear for parents, both liberal and conservative, in part because they stand as sites of youth autonomy, physical and psychological spaces beyond parental control.

Conclusion

In diverse societies, there is always a subjective, contested element in the definition of social issues. Definitions of social problems depend on the moral and social stances of those who are able to do the defining. Definitions are constructed through a range of processes involving relations of power. Definitions of actions as deviant, criminal, or wrong may be based on morals and values that are not widely shared. The notion of deviance itself implies disagreement over norms.

The state legislation of morality involves practices of what is often described as moral regulation, the government establishment of right and wrong, good and bad. Moral regulation encourages certain forms of conduct and expression while discouraging others. To do so, states establish disciplinary regimes, including systems of reward and punishment. Moral regulation can be carried out through state practices such as finance, taxation, social policy, and citizenship itself. Moral regulation is carried out in nearly every aspect of state practice.

References

Agamben, Giorgio. 2000. *Means Without End: Notes on Politics*. Minneapolis: University of Minnesota Press.

Amnesty International. 2004. *Stolen Sisters*. Ottawa: Amnesty International.

Anderson, Nels. 1923. *The Hobo: The Sociology of the Homeless Man*. Chicago: University of Chicago Press.

Bandura, Albert. 1977. *Social Learning Theory*. Morristown, NJ: General Learning Press.

Baylor Institute for Studies of Religion. 2008. "Survey".

Becker, Howard. 1963. *Outsiders: Studies in the Sociology of Deviance*. New York: Free Press.

Bramham, Daphne. 2008. "Actions Speak Much Louder Than Words: Aboriginal Women Need to be Empowered for First Nations to Break the Cycle of Poverty and Despair." *The Vancouver Sun,* Saturday, June 14.

Brennan, Luann. 2003. *Restoring the Justice in Criminal Justice*. Detroit: Wayne State University, Department of Interdisciplinary Studies.

Brock, D. 1998. *Making Work, Making Trouble: Prostitution as a Social Problem*. Toronto: University of Toronto Press.

Brooks, Carolyn. 2002. "Globalization and a New Underclass of 'Disposable People'." In *Marginality and Condemnation*, eds. Bernard Schissel and Carolyn Brooks. Halifax: Fernwood, 273-288.

Burt, Martha R. 1992. *Over the Edge: The Growth of Homelessness in the 1980s*. Thousand Oaks: Sage.

Canadian Press. 2008. "Court Strikes Down Victorian Bylaw Against Homeless Camping." October 14. http://www.cbc.ca/canada/british-columbia/story/2008/10/14/bc-victoria-homeless-bylaw.html

Carre J.M. and C.M. McCormick. 2008. "In Your Face: Facial Metrics Predict Behavioural Aggression in the Laboratory and in Varsity and Professional Ice Hockey Players." *Proceedings of the Royal Society: Biological Sciences* 275: 2651-2656.

Carre J.M., C.M. McCormick, and C.J. Mondloch. 2009. "Facial Structure is a Reliable Cue of Aggressive Behavior." *Psychological Science* 20: 1194-1198.

Center on Housing Rights and Evictions. 2007. *Mega Events and Olympics*. Geneva: COHRE.

Chan, Cheryl. 2009. "Police Bid to Reduce Civil Disorder on Streets Under Fire." *The Province*. February 15. http://www.theprovince.com/story_print.html?id=1293477&sponsor=

Cohen, Albert. 1955. *Delinquent Boys*. New York: Free Press.

Cohen, Stanley. 1973. *Folk Devils and Moral Panics*. London: Paladin.

Corbett, J. and J. Winebrake. 2010. "The Role of International Policy in Mitigating Global Shipping Emissions." *Brown Journal of World Affairs 2010* 16(2): 143-154.

———2007a. "Ship Pollution Death Toll 60,000." *Portwatch* 1-2.

———2007b. "Sustainable Movement of Goods: Energy and Environmental Implications of Trucks, Trains, Ships, and Planes." *Environmental Management* November: 8-12.

Dembicki, Geoff. 2009. "Homeless Relocations Part of 2010 Games Security Plan." *The Tyee*. March 26. http://thetyee.ca/Blogs/TheHook/Olympics2010/2009/03/26/homeless-relocations-2010-security/

Duchesne, Doreen. 1997. "Street Prostitution in Canada." *Juristat* 17 (2), Statistics Canada Catalogue 85-002-XPE.

Elias, Norbert. 1978. *The Civilizing Process*. Oxford: Blackwell.

Fedec, Kari. 2002. "Women and Children in Canada's Sex Trade: The Discriminatory Policing of the Marginalized." In *Marginality and Condemnation*, eds. Bernard Schissel and Carolyn Brooks. Halifax: Fernwood, 253-272.

Fletcher, Tom. 2008. "Circus Tents Won't Help the Homeless." *Surrey/North Delta Leader* October 22, 8.

Foucault, Michel. 1976. *The History of Sexuality Vol. 1: The Will to Knowledge*. London: Penguin.

———1975. *Discipline and Punish: the Birth of the Prison*, New York: Random House.

Gabor, Thomas. 1994. *Everybody Does It!: Crime by the Public*. Toronto: University of Toronto Press.

Gerdes, L. I., ed. 2004. *Endangered Oceans*. San Diego: Greenhaven Press.

Gilchrest, L. and R.A. Winchester. 1997. "Urban Survivors, Aboriginal Street Youth: Vancouver, Winnipeg and Montreal." In *For Seven Generations: An Information Legacy of the Royal Commission on Aboriginal Peoples*. Access Project. Institute of Indigenous Government. Ottawa: Ministry of Supply and Services.

Goff, Colin. 2004. *Criminal Justice in Canada*. Toronto: Thompson.

Grossman, J.R., A.D. Keating, and J.L. Reiff. 2005. *Encyclopedia of Chicago*. Chicago: University of Chicago Press.

Heathcote-James, Emma. 2002. *Seeing Angels*. London: John Blake Publishing.

Henry, Frances and Carol Tator. 2009. *The Colour of Democracy: Racism in Canadian Society*. Toronto: Pearson.

Hill, Mary Frances. 2009. "Downtown Eastside Residents Worry They'll be Jailed for Olympic Games." *The Vancouver Sun*. February 15. http://www.vancouversun.com/news/Downtown+Eastside+residents+worry+they+jailed+Olympic+Games/1293429/story.html

Kelling, George and James Q. Wilson. 1982. "Broken Windows: The Police and Neighborhood Safety." *Atlantic Monthly* 249(3): 29-38.

Kerner Commission. 1968. *Report of the National Advisory Commission on Civil Disorders*. New York: Bantam.

Khee-Jin Tan, A. 2006. *Vessel-Source Marine Pollution: The Law and Politics of International Regulation*. Cambridge: Cambridge University Press.

Laird, Gordon. 2007. *Homelessness in a Growth Economy: Canada's 21st Century Paradox*. Calgary: Sheldon Chumir Foundation for Ethics in Leadership.

Lanier, Mark M. and Stuart Henry. 2004. *Essential Criminology*. Boulder: Westview Press.

Leung, Wency. 2007. "Sex Workers Plan Brothel in 2010 Olympics City". *We-News*, October 11.

Lowman, J. 2000. "Violence and the Outlaw Status of (Street) Prostitution in Canada." *Violence Against Women* 9(6): 987-1011.

Lupick, 2008a. "Downtown Ambassadors Face Human Rights Complaint." *The Georgia Straight*. July 18. http://www.straight.com/node/154559

————2008b. "Security Guards 'Use Force Illegally' on Homeless, Pivot Legal Society Reports." *The Georgia Straight,* November 27. http://www.straight.com/article-173020/security-guards-%3F%3Fuse-force-illegally%3F%3F-homeless-pivot-legal-society-reports

Marx, Karl and Frederick Engels. 1970. *The German Ideology*. New York: International Publishers.

Melrose. M. 2003. "Street Prostitutes and Community Safety: A Case of Contested Meanings?" *Community Safety Journal* 1(2): 21-31.

Merton, Robert K. 1949. *Social Theory and Social Structure*. New York: Free Press.

Miles, Robert. 1993. *Racism after "Race Relations."* London: Routledge.

Mills, C. Wright. 1959. *The Sociological Imagination*. New York: Oxford University Press.

O'Grady, William. 2007. *Crime in Canadian Context: Debates and Controversies*. Don Mills: Oxford University Press.

Pew Forum on Religion and Public Life. 2007. *U.S. Religious Landscape Survey*.

Polk, K. and W. Schafer (eds.). 1972. *Schools and Delinquency*. Englewood Cliffs, NJ: Prentice-Hall.

Rieman, Jeffrey. 2006. *The Rich Get Richer and the Poor Get Prison: Ideology, Class and Criminal Justice*. Boston: Allyn and Bacon.

Royal Commission on Aboriginal Peoples. 1997. *For Seven Generations: An Information Legacy of the Royal Commission on Aboriginal Peoples*. Access Project. Institute of Indigenous Government. Ottawa: Ministry of Supply and Services.

Rousmaniere, K., K. Dehli, and N. de Coninck-Smith, eds. 1997. *Discipline, Moral Regulation and Schooling*. New York: Garland.

Shantz, Jeff, ed. 2011. *Law Against Liberty: The Criminalization of Dissent*. Lake Mary, Florida: Vandeplas Publishing.

———2010. *Constructive Anarchy: Building Infrastructures of Resistance*. Surrey: Ashgate.

Stark, Rodney. 2009. *What Americans Really Believe*. Waco: Baylor University Press.

Strange, Carolyn and Tina Loo. 1997. *Making Good: Law and Moral Regulation in Canada, 1867-1939*. Toronto: University of Toronto Press.

Sutherland, Edwin H. 1949. *White Collar Crime*. New York: Holt, Rinehart and Winston.

Swanson, Jean. 2001. *Poor Bashing: The Politics of Exclusion*. Toronto: Between the Lines.

Talouli, Anthony. n.d. "Addressing Shipping Related Marine Pollution in the Pacific Islands Region." http://www.sprep.org/solid_waste/marine.htm.

Taylor, Ian R., Paul Walton, and Jock Young. 1988. *The New Criminology: For a Social Theory of Deviance*. London: Routledge.

Taylor, R. and J. Covington. 1988. "Neighborhood Changes in Ecology and Violence." *Criminology* 26: 553-589.

Umbreit, Mark S., Robert B. Coates, Betty Vos, and Kathy Brown. 2002. *Victim Offender Dialogue in Crimes of Severe Violence: A Multi-Site Study of Programs in Texas and Ohio*. Minneapolis: Center for Restorative Justice, University of Minnesota.

UNEP. 2006. *Ecosystems and Biodiversity in Deepwaters and High Seas*. UNEP Regional Seas Report and Studies 178.

Vidal, John. 2009. "Health risks of shipping pollution have been 'underestimated'." *The Guardian*. April.

Weber, Max. 2002. *The Protestant Ethic and The Spirit of Capitalism*. London: Penguin Books.

White, Rob, Fiona Haines, and Lauren Eisler. 2009. *Crime and Criminology: An Introduction*. Toronto: Oxford.

Willis, Paul. 1977. *Learning to Labour: How Working Class Kids Get Working Class Jobs*. Aldershot: Gower.